WILLIAM VERRALL'S COOKERY BOOK

First published 1759

Edited by Ann Haly
With an Introduction by Colin Brent

SOUTHOVER PRESS
1988

First published in 1988 by
SOUTHOVER PRESS
2 Cockshut Road
Lewes, East Sussex BN7 1JH

Copyright © Title. William Verrall's Cookery Book
© Introduction. Colin Brent

British Library Cataloguing in Publication Data

Verrall, William, 1715 – 1761
 (A complete system of cookery). William
 Verrall's cookery book.
 1. Food—Recipes
 I. Title   II. Haly, Ann
 641.5

 ISBN 1 870962 00 1

Jacket designed by Andy Gammon
Phototypeset in Garamond 10/11½ pt
by Pauline Newton, Chichester

Printed in Great Britain by
Villiers Publications Ltd
26A Shepherds Hill
London N6 5AH

CONTENTS

SOURCES OF ILLUSTRATIONS

St Nicholas's Hospital, Lewes. Watercolour, James Lambert, Jnr. 1779. Cover. Sussex Archaeological Society, Lewes.

Lewes Castle, from J. V. Button, *The Brighton and Lewes Guide*. 1805. Sussex Archaeological Society, Lewes.

Salmon, sheep, sea tortoise, sea lobster, from Buffon *Natural History*. Abridged edition. Published by C. and G. Kearsley, Fleet St, London. 1791.

Teal, pheasant, rabbit from *The Natural History of Selbourne* by The Rev. Gilbert White. Orr and Smith, Paternoster Row, London. 1836.

Decorative engraving, from *The Poetical Works of J. Langhorne, D.D. with Life of the Author*. C. Cooke. 17 Paternoster Row, London. 1798.

Title page from the original edition of *A New System of Cookery*. 1759.

PREFACE

William Verrall wrote his lively cookery book to introduce the lighter more aristocratic style of cooking, which he had learned from the French cook St Clouet, to a wider public than his patrons of the *White Hart*, Lewes. La Varenne's book, *The French Cook*, had already been published in translation in 1653, one year after appearing in France, and French culinary ideas were gradually gaining ground although, of course, already well known to the wealthy few who kept a French cook. But such ideas had run into considerable opposition from English traditionalists when they began to be more widely disseminated in the first part of the eighteenth century. Indeed, Hannah Glasse in her *Art of Cookery*, published in 1747, complained bitterly about the extravagance of French receipts. The reforming style came into the repertoire nevertheless and its influence is to be found in the receipts of such well known cooks as Eliza Acton in the first half of the nineteenth century, and later, with yet more accretions, Isabella Beeton.

Verrall probably provided two separate menus at his inn: one for his more fashionable and sophisticated customers, and one for conservative eaters, as Colin Brent suggests in his Introduction. Thomas Turner, the mercer from East Hoathly, dined at the *White Hart* in 1756 on boiled beef and greens, a breast of veal roasted and a butter pudding cake — a solid, traditional meal.

vii

It was usual to serve two courses at dinner which was normally between three and five o'clock. A great many different dishes, corner dishes and side dishes were put on the table at the same time and the diners helped themselves by passing the dishes round. It was not until the nineteenth century that diners at an inn would have been waited on at table.

Cleanliness and proper equipment were also Verrall's concern. His story of the kitchen where Nanny worked, whether true or not, goes to show that dirt and disorder were probably to be found in most establishments of the time. They are not unknown today.

Here then are his receipts, the result of his apprenticeship and life as an innkeeper. Nearly all of them can be used today, with a little experiment to reduce the quantities for a small family. Some are not to our taste — few of us would want to eat a dish of calves' eyes cooked the same way as their brains, or clean and cook a whole turtle. Some are familiar, mackerel broiled with herbs, for instance. Many reintroduce a range of flavours that are unusual, such as cucumber fried gently in butter as an accompaniment to mutton, or the lamb that we eat now, and hard-boiled eggs with a little cullis and sweet herbs. His receipts for fruit fritters are well worth reviving; the Bavarian apple fritters are particularly good. A number are very cheap and excellent, among them Collops of Rabbit and Hogs' Ears à la St Menhoult — this last interesting receipt is very much more delicious than it sounds. The receipts for vegetables as an integral part of the main course show some forgotten ways of using them, parsley roots with chicken and lambs' ears with sorrel, for example. In short, this is a cookery book to be used as much as read as an historical curiosity.

The patrons of the *White Hart* are to be envied their enthusiastic innkeeper. It must have been something of a culinary experience to eat there.

The varied French and English spelling is his own, as is the punctuation. I have altered the order slightly for easier reading.

ANN HALY

ACKNOWLEDGEMENTS

I am indebted to the Sussex Archaeological Society who gave me access to the 1759 text of William Verrall's *A New System of Cookery*, and for their permission to reproduce James Lambert, Junior's, watercolour of St Nicholas's Hospital, Lewes, and Lewes Castle, from J. V. Button's *Brighton and Lewes Guide*. In particular I would like to thank Joyce Crow, Honorary Librarian of the Society, as well as Dorothy Brown, Kenneth Dickens, John Houghton and Fiona Marsden. I am grateful to Eunice Kemp, Ian Clifton, and Alan Shelley, all of whom gave up valuable time to answer my questions. And to Tom Reeves for his splendid photography. I am also grateful to many others, too numerous to mention here, who have given this project enthusiasm, interest and support.

INTRODUCTION

William Verrall's *A Complete System of Cookery* anticipates another such classic — John Fothergill's *An Innkeeper's Diary*. Both men wrote in alert, sinewy and amusing prose of their passion for culinary perfection in the arduous context of innkeeping. And despite William's pose as 'a poor publican', his *White Hart* at Lewes was a very substantial hostelry, and even more rooted in the life of a market town and its region than Fothergill's *Spread Eagle* at Thame. And by a nice coincidence Fothergill also lived in Lewes (well before he donned buckled shoes and turned innkeeper) as secretary-cum-apprentice to Edward Perry Warren, an American connoisseur of Hellenistic sculpture and the pelvic curve, whose gift of Rodin's *The Kiss* to the Town Council was prudishly refused.

Refronted in the 1840s, the *White Hart Hotel* still stands in Lewes High Street, just opposite the neo-classical Crown Courts, formerly the County Hall of Sussex. Its internal layout, along with some fireplaces and panelling, dates back to Elizabeth's reign, when the Pelhams of Laughton (the gentry ancestors of William's august patron, the Duke of Newcastle) used the mansion as a town house. Shortly before 1724 William's father Richard converted the premises into a capacious and well appointed hostelry, as a finely penned inventory, drawn up at his death in 1737, reveals. A balconied 'Great Room' upstairs boasted four tables, 25 chairs and fifteen sconces. Behind lay a billiard room, a club room hung with eleven prints, and three best bedrooms, embellished with green, blue or yellow 'china' furniture. A dozen more bedsteads cluttered the garrets. Downstairs were a parlour, 'the old hall and bar', kitchens, a buttery, a brewhouse, and stables large enough to be supplied with 'ten dozen halters'. In the garden stood twelve posts and wires for drying clothes. Other accessories included six china plates, eight Delft plates, 82 pewter dishes, copper coffee and chocolate pots, 30 wheatear pots, 33 decanters, 20 punch bowls with ladles, and a regiment of chamberpots, pewter or white. The barrels of mild and strong beer were valued at five guineas, and the hogsheads of red and white port wine at £29.

Richard Verrall had prospered along with the *White Hart*, to judge from his 'wearing apparell and money in purse' worth £220, and his recoverable 'bonds, bills and book debts' worth £923 19s. A thousand pounds was a solid personal estate in early Georgian England. The inn's success, of course, owed something to Lewes's busy commerce. The Saturday market drew wealthy sheep-and-corn farmers from as far as Eastbourne. Breweries and malthouses abounded. Great livestock fairs were held on St Mark's Day, Whit Tuesday, and St Matthew's Day. By the bridge over the river Ouse barges from Newhaven unloaded groceries, spices, cheese, wine and textiles from London, and sea-coal from Newcastle, for shopkeepers many miles around. They returned downstream with local wheat, barley, timber, iron and ordnance. Such commerce brought custom to the inn, and ensured a flow of varied ingredients to its kitchens. Also readily available were sea-fish from Brighton, salmon, trout and eels from the Ouse, wild fowl from the adjacent marshland, crammed poultry from the weald, and vast downland flocks of wheatears, which, fresh or potted, endlessly seduced the contemporary palate.

Besides commerce and ingredients, Lewes also thrived on administration. Magistrates from the Rapes of Lewes, Pevensey and Hastings held their quarter sessions there, dealing with misdemeanours and with the complexities of poor relief, bastardy and settlement. Churchwardens from Lewes archdeaconry were sworn in each Easter at St Michael's church (where William was baptised, married and buried), and litigants brought tithe disputes and probate matters to the archdeacon's court close by. And from all six rapes of Sussex, the county's elite (the landowners, clergy and freeholders) assembled at Lewes, for the race meeting in August, for the biennial summer visit of the assize judges, closely attended by trumpeters and the high sheriff, and for the election of two county MPs, held in the ruins of the Norman castle. Lewes's lawyers, doctors, schoolmasters and musicians, serviced this converging elite, as did the elegant bedrooms and well stocked cellars of the *White Hart*.

Already tapping Lewes's prosperity were the *Star* and the *White Horse*, equally capacious hostelries, and both well established there in 1724. But the *White Hart* enjoyed a unique advantage, to which the 'Club Room' listed in the 1737 inventory offers a clue. The club that caroused there every Wednesday was subsidised by the Duke of Newcastle, the county's greatest magnate, whose many, and loyal, Pelham relatives, collectively known as 'the Family', ramified across eastern Sussex. Moreover, such was the political power consolidated at Westminster by Newcastle and his brother Henry, that upon Walpole's departure first Henry, and then the Duke, served as Prime Minister, from 1743 to 1762. To elect his candidates at Seaford, Hastings, Winchelsea and Rye, the Duke relied on hard cash, feasts, and the promise of a job in government service. But Lewes, with its large and alert electorate, needed steadier nursing, and in particular a campaign headquarters, where the Duke's partisans could roister at his expense. To meet this need, the ancient mansion in the High Street, owned by a Pelham cousin, was converted into the *White Hart*.

Thus the Duke and 'the Family' footed stupendous bills for wine, spirits, beer, broken glasses and fireworks, consumed at the inn during the long months of bitter campaigning that preceded the Lewes elections of 1727 and 1734. After canvassing the borough or attending the races (which came to the same thing), the Duke relaxed in the billiard room, fitted up at his own expense, and doubtless available to his cronies in the club room next door. But he slept off the premises, in another Elizabethan mansion close by, which Nicholas Dubois had recently Palladianized for his Pelham cousin (now Pelham House).

Besides managing the *White Hart*, Richard Verrall also obliged the Duke by serving as High Constable of Lewes in 1719, 1729 and 1734. Embracing as it did the role of returning officer for the borough, this position gave free play to partiality at election time. And in 1734 Newcastle chose the eldest of Richard's seven sons, also Richard, to preside over a coffee house (now Newcastle House), newly opened just opposite the *White Hart*. With assembly rooms *en suite*, the coffee house offered a more decorous setting for mixed company than did the inn. As Steward of Lewes races, Newcastle channelled to young Richard there the handicapping of entries for the King's Plate etc. All three amenities, of course (inn, coffee house and assembly rooms), catered for the Duke's supporters among the county elite, when they thronged into Lewes for the races, the assizes and county elections, and this further advantaged the *White Hart* in its early fight for custom.

Given the inn's political importance, the Duke and 'the Family' doubtless took great pains over choosing a successor, when Richard senior died in 1737. His sons were obvious candidates. Richard junior was managing the coffee house. Edward, bookseller and stationer, had just finely penned his father's inventory. Henry was to follow Richard at the coffee house in 1742, where he presided 'with an equal share of respectability and profit' till 1779. But the choice fell on William, the fourth son, who celebrated his twenty-second birthday in April of that year. His selection at so early an age for so responsible a task presumably owed much to his having trained in the Duke's own kitchens — a privilege probably solicited by his father. The ducal household mostly divided its time between Newcastle House in Lincoln's Inn Fields and Claremont, a princely mansion near Esher, enlarged by Vanbrugh and demolished by Clive of India. (The Belvedere survives, along with William Kent's amphitheatre, island temple and grotto, in the care of the National Trust.) Amid such splendours the Duke feasted his fellow Whig oligarchs, and his French cook, 'Monsieur de St Clouet', with whom William 'served his Time', naturally enjoyed an international reputation. In the 1750s he returned to France in the entourage of the British ambassador, before joining the household of Marechal Richelieu.

On settling in at the *White Hart*, William began straight away to practise cuisine 'after the French Method', or so the *Lewes Journal* assures us. Quite probably, though, the rank-and-file of Newcastle's supporters retained a stolid distaste for any dish more subtle than potted wheatear — the caucus carousing in the club room, or the 133 'determined voters' who massed for a borough by-election in 1738, or the seventy freeholders who dined with Lord Middlesex, a candidate for the county, in 1741. More promising were the landowners and clergy who continued to pack the 'Great Room' upstairs during the races, the assizes and county elections. And as his preface makes clear, William was often summoned to the kitchens of the neighbouring gentry (at Stanmer, Firle, Glynde and Glyndebourne presumably), where he proselytized the cooks and triumphed over the 'apparatus'. Even in Lewes he won disciples among the higher bourgeoisie. So it was *A System*, embodying over twenty years of practice, that William published in 1759. And that year itself was rather apt, being the *annus mirabilis*, the year of victories, of Guadaloupe, Minden, Quebec, Lagos, Quiberon Bay and Madras, and the political apogee of his steadfast patron, the Duke of Newcastle, still reigning at the Treasury.

Like their father, William and his brothers obliged the Duke by serving as High Constable, five times between 1737 and 1765. In return their widowed mother Sarah secured the Duke's promise, at the conveniently public Lewes races, of a post in 'the

Treasury, Customs, War, Pay or Stamp Office' for their brother Charles. Opting instead to keep the *George and Dragon* at Arundel, he resurrected the pledge in a letter to Newcastle eighteen years later. By then widow Sarah had importuned another 'little Place', for her youngest son Manfield, who had failed in business and become 'a Dead Weight' on the family resources. Brother Edward, too, feeling menaced as a bookseller by the new circulating libraries, secured a Surveyorship of Windows. William, of course, was already deeply indebted to the Duke. Nevertheless, when the Lewes postmaster died in 1740, he angled hopefully to 'fix' the business at the *White Hart*, and although the franchise turned out to be already promised to Edward Tasker, the perukemaker next door, William did secure the carriage of letters between Lewes and Eastbourne, which then enjoyed no direct postal link with London.

William's business at the *White Hart* increased in other ways. His brother George held auctions there. In 1760 the magistrates conducted quarter sessions in the 'Great Room', while their Sessions House was rebuilt outside. Stage coach traffic appeared, once the turnpike trusts improved the main roads between Brighton, Lewes and London, via Chailey or Uckfield, in the mid-1750s. As the *Lewes Journal* noted, his stables could stall a hundred horses; and by 1762 the 'Lewes & Brighton New Flying Machine', neat, commodious and hung on steel springs, was shuttling between Charing Cross, the *White Hart* and the *Castle* at Brighton three times weekly. But by then the inn was under new management. In February 1761 William's furniture was put up for auction, including 'the Brewing Copper, about 170 gallons', and in March he was declared bankrupt. The very same month, having married Hannah Turner on the 2nd, he died, being buried on the 26th. In July Thomas Scrase took the inn and remained till 1791. In August crowds thronged there to consult the celebrated itinerant oculist, Chevalier John Taylor, whose surgery, although allegedly efficacious in 80,000 cases, had recently killed J. S. Bach.

The circumstances of William's bankruptcy and death are unclear. Only a few weeks before, he solicited the long-suffering Newcastle for 'a Place', and the Duke responded (while conducting a global war) with the Keepership of Middlesex House of Correction. Unless the whippings and allied duties were to be performed by an energetic proxy, this offer does not suggest failing health as a cause of his bankruptcy, and rather rules out his marriage to Hannah Turner being a mere romantic gesture. Perhaps the swelling business at the *White Hart* simply engulfed him. Perhaps the death of his first wife in 1757 robbed him of an essential helpmate. Entrepreneurship among some Verralls was, after all, shakily founded; Manfield became a 'Dead Weight'; Edward was haunted by circulating libraries; and Charles renounced the *George and Dragon* at Arundel, to become a well-known recluse in a purpose-built 'New Jerusalem' at Warning-camp. Perhaps, too, his passion for cuisine 'after the French Method' seduced him too often from prosaic routines. If so, then this new edition of his *magnum opus* will at least serve as an abiding memorial.

COLIN BRENT

Many biographical details of William Verrall, his father, his brothers and a sister, were meticulously set out by Perceval Lucas in his article on 'The Verrall Family Of Lewes', published in volume 58 of the *Sussex Archaeological Collections*. Lucas made excellent use of the voluminous correspondence of Thomas Pelham-Holles, Duke of Newcastle (1693 – 1768), now in the British Library, which the author has explored further. The Duke's political and artistic patronage has recently been examined by Nicholas Thompson in *A House In Town: 22 Arlington Street, Its Owners and Builders* (Batsford, 1984). The inventory of the *White Hart*, drawn up in June 1737, resides in the East Sussex Record Office at Lewes (INV 2697).

A

COMPLETE SYSTEM

OF

COOKERY.

In which is set forth,

A Variety of genuine RECEIPTS,
collected from several Years Experience
under the celebrated Mr. de St. CLOUET,
sometime since COOK to his Grace the
Duke of *Newcastle*.

By WILLIAM VERRAL,
Master of the *White-Hart* Inn in *Lewes*, *Sussex*.

Together with an INTRODUCTORY PREFACE,

Shewing how every Dish is brought to Table,
and in what Manner the meanest Capacity shall
never err in doing what his Bill of Fare con-
tains.

To which is added,

A true Character of Monf. de St. CLOUET.

LONDON,
Printed for the AUTHOR, and sold by him;
As also by EDWARD VERRAL Bookseller, in *Lewes*:
And by JOHN RIVINGTON in *St. Paul's Church-yard, London*.

M DCC LIX.

WILLIAM VERRALL'S PREFACE

From a presumption of some small success from my friends
I venture to publish the following treatise. To pretend to write
for fame would illy become a person in my sphere of life (who
am no more than what is vulgarly called a poor publican).
'Twould be an unparalleled piece of imprudence, and wholly
incompatible to reason and the nature of things. 'Twill be
sufficient for me that it meets with the approbation amongst my
friends and acquaintances, as may just satisfy me for the pains
I have taken to collect them (though small matters) together. The
chief end and design of this part of my little volume is to show,
both to the experienced and unexperienced in the business, the
whole and simple art of the most modern and best French
Cookery; to lay down before them such an unerring guide how
it may always be well managed, and please the eye as well as the
taste of everybody; and to show, too, by the notorious errors
I have frequently seen, how of course it must for ever fail of being
either good or pleasing, and a great many favourite morsels
entirely spoiled.

First, then, give me leave to advise those who please to try
the following receipts, to provide a proper apparatus for the work
they take in hand, without which it is impossible it can be done
with the least air of decency: and before I finish this, shall further
show by maxims unexceptionable, that a good dinner cannot be

got up to look neat and pretty without proper utensils to work it in, such as neat stewpans of several sizes, soup-pots, &c. to do it withal, though your provisions be never so good. I have been sent for many and many a time to get dinners for some of the best families hereabouts; the salute generally is: Will, (for that is my name) I want you to dress me a dinner to-day; with all my heart, Sir, says I; how many will your company be; why about ten or twelve, or thereabouts: and what would you please to have me get, Sir, for ye? O, says the gentleman, I shall leave that entirely to you; but I'll show you my larder, and you'll be the better judge how to make your bill of fare; and a vast plenty of good provisions there was, enough to make two courses, one of seven, the other of nine, with an addition only of three or four small dishes for the second course; and a fine dish of fish there was for a remove. So it was agreed that should be the thing; but, says the gentleman, be sure you make us some good things in your own way, for they are polite sort of gentry that are to dine with me. I promised my care, and wrote the bill immediately; and it was vastly approved of. My next step was to go and offer a great many compliments to Mrs. Cook about getting the dinner; and as it was her master's order I should assist her, I hoped we should agree; and the girl, I'll say that for her, returned the compliment very prettily, by saying, Sir, whatever my master or you shall order me to do, shall be done as far and as well as I am able. But Nanny (for that I found to be her name) soon got into such an air as often happens upon such occasions. Pray, Nanny, says I, where do you place your stewpans, and the other things you make use of in the cooking way? La, Sir, says she, that is all we have (pointing to one poor solitary stewpan, as one might call it,) but no more fit for the use than a wooden hand-dish. Ump, says I to myself, how's this to be? A surgeon may as well attempt to make an incision with a pair of sheers, or open a vein with an oyster-knife, as for me to pretend to get this dinner without proper tools to do it; here's neither stewpan, soup-pot, or any one thing else that is useful; there's what they call a frying-pan indeed, but black as my hat, and a handle long enough to obstruct half the passage of the kitchen. However, upon a little pause I sent away post haste for my own kitchen furniture. In the meantime Nanny and I kept on in preparing what we could, that no time might be lost. When the things came we at it again, and all was in a tolerable way, and forward enough for the time of day; but at length wanting a sieve I begg'd of Nanny to give me one, and so she did in a moment; but such a one!—I put my fingers to it and found it gravelly. Nanny, says I, this won't do, it is sandy: she look'd at it, and angry enough she was: rot our Sue, says she, she's always taking my sieve to sand her nasty dirty stairs. But, however, to be a little cleanly Nanny gave it a good thump upon the table, much about the part of it where the meat is generally laid, and whips it into the boiler where I suppose the pork and cabbage was boiling for the family, gives it a sort of a rinse, and gave it me again, with as much of the pork fat about it as would poison the whole dinner; so I said no more, but could not use it, and made use of a napkin that I slily made friends with her fellow-servant for; at which she leer'd round and set off; but I heard her say as she flirted her tail into the scullery, hang these men cooks, they are so confounded nice.—I'll be whipt, says she, if there was more sand in the sieve than would lay upon a sixpence. However, she came again presently, and I soon coax'd her into good humour again; come, says I, Nanny, I'm going to make a fricasee of chickens, observe how I cut 'em (for I'll show ye how to do any part of the dinner), and she seemed very attentive. When I had cut mine, there, says I, do you take that, and cut it in the same manner: and indeed the girl handled her knife well, and did it very prettily: then I gave her directions how to proceed; and it was done neatly, notwithstanding the story of the sandy sieve. I then took in hand to show her in what manner it was to be finished for the table. And now, dinner being dish'd up, Nanny was vastly pleased, and said, that in her judgment it was the prettiest and best she had ever seen. When 'twas over, the gentleman desired, if I had time in the evening, he should be glad

I would come and get him two or three little matters for supper, for they all stay: and be sure, says he, make us just such another fricasee, for it was highly approved on; so I went and told Nanny she should do it; which was agreed to: but, Sir, says she, if I don't do right I hope you'll tell me. But it was done to my mind, and Nanny was now the cook; supper was sent in, and great praises ran from plate to plate, and they unanimously agreed that that fricasee was better than what they had for dinner. Before supper was well over out comes the gentleman to me. Will, says he, we hope you have this dish in the book you are going to publish. Yes, Sir, says I, and everything else you had to-day drest in the foreign way. But, Sir, says I, your cook did that you had for supper. My maid do it, says he, and away he went to his company. Nanny was immediately sent for, and after some questions something was given her for the care she had taken; so I wished the family a good night, and went home. The next day, just as I had finished the transcribing my first sheet for the press, in comes an elderly gentleman, a friend of mine, and took it up to read. While I was writing on he interrupted me, by asking what was meant by apparatus, here, this word says he, (holding it to me to read). Why, Sir, says I, it comprehends all necessary and useful things for dressing a dinner fit to serve a gentleman's table, particularly your pretty little made dishes, (what are generally called French dishes). Ump, says my old friend, I seldom eat any thing more than a mutton chop, or so; but, however, 'tis all very well for them that like it. Well, but Sir, says I, please to give me leave; I take it you must have a good handsome kitchen in your great house, and well furnished I suppose. Not a jot, says my good friend, not a jot, I want none. Why, Sir, says I, gentlemen in general are as well pleased with the handsome decorations of their kitchen (though they never dress a morsel of victuals there) as they are with an expensive and fine furnished parlour. Well, says he, I like your scheme very well; but what must I get? So I named several things, and their uses. Well, I'll go and see, says he, and away he went cock-a-hoop to the brazier's immediately, and buys much about as much as is necessary for the getting up such a dinner as I sent to table yesterday; which is enough for any private gentleman's family, or the best inn or tavern in England; and costs but a trifle, (for I had seen it without the old gentleman's knowing it). But in he comes to tell me what he had done, and seemed mightily pleased that I approved on't, and invited me to come to see it to-morrow. Next day I went, and was had into the kitchen by my old friend, and very neat and decent it look'd; but when I had gazed round a little, talking of his admirable taste of placing his furniture, I missed one material article, which put me in mind of an observation I have made, and often seen in small country houses; you may be sure to find a mantelpiece with spits, a hold-fast, basting-ladle, drudging-box, iron skewers, &c., but you may look all over the house and find no jack; just such is the case of my good neighbour Hackum, he seems so delighted with his new show that he lives in the kitchen, and chuses it rather than his parlour, but has not thought one word of a stove; so I addressed myself to him, while walking round by way of pleasing him, I presume, Sir, your stoves are in your back kitchen, in the old fashion way; stoves, says he, what d'ye mean by stoves? Why, Sir, little round machines of iron fix'd in brickwork about three feet from the ground, where charcoal is always burnt on all occasions in the cooking way, without which all your other materials are of no sort of use but as you see 'em now. Oh no, says he, it mayn't be often I shall invite my friends, and when I do my maid can do it all very well over this fire. (Now the fire-place, to save coals, is reduced to about the size of a salt-box.) After a little more chat about indifferent things I bid the old gentleman good-morrow, and trudged home; but dare say I shall hear from him again about the stoves, and some other little matters there must be added to it that will surprize him again, but all not worth naming. As I said so it happened, for the old man was close at my heels, and without ceremony of any sort, Will, says he, I'll have my stoves put up to-morrow, and next day I'll invite a few friends to try how my furniture answers;

you'll come and dress my dinner for me, won't you? Yes, Sir, with a vast deal of pleasure. Well, says he, there will be about four of us, three of which was with him, I think, an attorney's clerk, a taylor, and a journeyman perriwig-maker, who, I suppose, are much about as great epicures as himself. What do you please I should get you, Sir, says I? Why, um, says he, I don't know, I think I have heard you talk of five and five, and a remove. Now, says he, I should think three and three and two removes would be better. (Ay, says I to myself, put two fresh dishes upon the table, and leave one tore all to pieces to keep up the symmetry of it.) Just as you like, Sir, says I, and for novelty-sake so 'tis to be. Now he ordered me to provide just what I thought proper; only that he should be glad of a soup-maigre; and then set off. Now I heard him say to his cronies, as he went along, I know I shall like that soup-maigre because they always stuff it full of meat. Maigre, says he, I suppose is French for meat; so in English we may call it a meat-soup. I went to market next morning, and provided what I judged necessary for their dinners, and took care to get enough; for I supposed 'em to be good trenchermen; and about one o'clock dinner went up, the soup, three fowls and bacon, and a large shoulder of mutton. The soup they eat all up, which was a very large old-fashioned pewter dish full; then fell aboard of the fowls, and demolished them, and so on to the mutton; but before they had finished it a dispute arose about what meat the soup was made of. Beef and bacon to be sure, says my old friend (and kept on eating like a ploughman). His right-hand man said he thought it was composed of *rumps and burs. He at the bottom took it to be made of a leg of mutton and turnips. Well, Sir, says he, to one upon the left, what think you of it? Why, Sir, I won't think of it at all: if I do I shall be sick, for I have eat too much of it. At length they sent for me, and I decided it; which surprized them. There was no other ingredients than about six carrots, as many turnips, and onions and herbs boiled to a sort

*Rumps and burs are the tails flea'd, and roots of the ears of a bullock; common perquisite of a journeyman-butcher, or tanner.

of porridge, and strained through a cullender to a large quantity
of toasted bread: the next three things were a hare, a turkey, (both
baked, and spoiled, for want of a proper fire in the kitchen) and
a plumb-pudding. There was no ceremony for clean plates; but
at it they went, just as they do at one of our country club-feasts;
the turkey was stript in a minute, and the poor hare tore all to
pieces, (for there was not a carver amongst them) and a most pro-
found silence there was for a long time, except only a very pretty
concert of growling, smacking their chaps, and cracking of crusts:
when all was over with meat, plates were called for the pudding,
which disappeared in about three minutes, though no small one.
The two removes, as the old gentleman called them, were then
brought in, and the question was which should be taken off? The
empty dish, says one; and that they all agreed to. Take away the
turkey, says the tonsor. No, says another, the hare; so as they
could not agree, a third took the hare and plunged it into the
turkey's dish. The removes were then put on; and that the beauty
of the third course (as I call it) might be kept up, at each end was
a sort of pudding, and in the middle the gibbet of the hare, and
the skeleton of the turkey. Now the two puddings (improperly
called so) were made as follows: I took a few potatoes, boiled,
and thump'd to pieces, with an egg or two, and a little sugar,
for one; the other was a few old mackeroons I had in my house
perhaps twenty years: I soak'd 'em well, and put them into a little
milk and flour, instead of cream and eggs, seasoned it high with
plenty of onions, &c., to which I added a large clove of garlick,
which is enough for the dishes of a fifty-cover table served twice
over, and covered it over with some good old Cheshire cheese
instead of Parmesan; so that the colours were alike, and sent up,
as said before. Well, neighbour, says the old gentleman, now for
a bit of pudding, and then we shall have done pretty well, I hope:
let's see, here's eight of us; so they were cut into so many parts,
and every one took his share, and heartily they fell to, except
one whose taste was not quite so depraved as the rest; he tasted,
but went no farther. You don't eat, neighbour, says the opposite

gentleman. I don't love sweet things, says he. Well, I do, says one that was gobbling down the highest dish that ever was. They vastly commended it, and swallowed it all down; but the beauty of it was, the mackeroon eaters eat it for a custard, and to this moment call it the best they ever tasted. But one of 'em said it had a terrible twang of a bad egg, though there was neither egg or butter in it. Well, says my old friend, with such a sort of a groan as may frequently be heard in large peals at your great feasts in and about the metropolis of this kingdom. I say, I hope every body has made a good dinner; but we may thank you for it, Mr. Cook, says he, turning to me; why we should have cut but a sad figure to-day, if we had not had the apparatusses. Pray, Sir, says one of the most learned, what is an apparatus? Why, says my old friend, laughing at him, why a stewpan is one, a pot is another, a ladle another, and many other things down in my kitchen are called apparatusses; so I left them in the midst of their sublime chat, and went home, where, to my no great surprize, I found the gentleman whose dinner I dress'd t'other day. Will, says he, why here you have made a strange racket at our house. My maid talks of nothing but you; what a pretty dinner you sent to table, and so easy, that it seemed no more trouble to ye than for her to make a Welch rabbit; but says, that if she had such a set of kitchen goods as yours, and a little of your instructions, she could do it all very well. Well, Sir, says I, if you please to furnish such things as are wanting, and spare a little of her time to peruse what I am about to publish, I make no doubt but she'll make an excellent cook. The girl is in the right on't, she told me she was afraid you would set her a spel by and by, by ordering just such another dinner, and I am sure it is impossible two made dishes can be well done with what your kitchen affords. What must I do then, says he, Will? Why has not your good old neighbour Hackum invited ye to see his kitchen since he has furnished it? No, says he. Well, he has got all quite new from top to bottom; such a set as will just do for you; and I'll tell you what it is, and then shall draw to a conclusion; but must ask the favour of one small digression.—I promised at the beginning to fix one never-erring chart to steer by, so that the weakest capacity shall never do amiss, though he mayn't arrive at once to that pitch of perfection equal to that of the celebrated Mons. Clouet. First then, my brethren, take care to begin your work betimes. Your broth and gravy for your soups and sauces should be the first thing in hand: your little matters in the pastry way may be done whilst that is going on; next prepare your fowls, collops, cutlets, or whatever it may be; put them upon plates, and range them in neat order upon the dresser before ye; next see that your meat and roast in the English way be all cleverly trimmed, trussed and singed, and ready for the spit. In like manner get all your garden things cut, pared, pick'd, and washed out into a cullender; and amongst the rest be sure you provide a plate of green onions, shallots, parsley, minced very fine, pepper and salt always ready mixed, and your spice-box always at hand; so that every thing you want may be ready at a moment's call, and not to be hunting after such trifles when your dinner should be ready to send to table. When your stewpans, &c., make their appearance, place them all in proper arrangement, and you cannot easily err. (For want of this steady care I have known a whole course stopt, and the half of a very grand dinner in a fair way of being spoiled by misplacing only one stewpan, and the cooks (though great ones) were forced to make shift with any thing they could throw together to make a dish to fill the chasm on the table; but it was found out at last that the poor scullery woman finding it among the foul things without looking under the cover, soust it into the dishkeeler, and 'twas lost. It was only a charming dish of green morels, in the room of which was served six or eight heads of celery flung into a frying-pan for a little colour, and dished up with a little sugar sifted over it.) What I observed before this long parenthesis I call good management, and will always succeed; the reverse of it is bad. I have known the time more than once or twice, that a cook has loitered away his time in the morning, and began his work perhaps at ten o'clock, and then at the wrong end too: so that time has so elapsed upon his hands that it was impossible for him to be ready at the hour set for sending to table; so that instead of winning the praises of his master or lady, and the rest of the good company, he gets into disgrace, and loses his character. This is what is meant by saying the cook can never do well, for they must fail of it if they are regardless of time, so take it by the forelocks, my friends, and follow the instructions in the treatise before ye, and you'll be sure to be right, and soon procure to yourself a vast deal of fame. Now, Sir, please to give me leave to make a catalogue of such things as you stand in need of in your kitchen: Two little boilers, one big enough for your broth or boiling a leg of mutton, and the other for the boiling of a couple of fowls or so, a soup-pot, eight small stewpans of different sizes, two very large ones, and covers to them all, a neat handy frying pan that may serve as well for frying any little matters, as an amlette or pancakes, a couple of copper ladles, two or three large copper spoons, a slice, or two, and an egg spoon, all tinn'd; a pewter cullender, three or four sieves, (one of lawn); to which you may add half a dozen copper cups that hold about three-fourths of half a pint, and as many of a lesser size, and an *etamine or two for the straining your thick soups, cullies or creams. Your cook will find uses for all these utensils, if you should ever give an order to get the dishes prescribed in the following receipts: but all your wooden ladles, skimmers, cabbage-nets, and such nasty things, banish them from your kitchen, let them not touch your broth, soup, fish, or any thing else; keep nothing of that sort there but two or three large wooden spoons, and them always kept clean for their particular uses, such as stirring any of your sauces in your stewpans, for pewter will melt, and copper will fret the tinning off. It is needless to say any thing of little round sauce-pans for venison sauce, warming of gravy, melting of butter or fish sauce, or the like. 'Tis supposed every house has a provision of that sort. And now let my brother or sister cook come

*An etamine is a fluff made on purpose for these uses, and are sold at many shops in London.

on clean and neat like my friend and patron Clouet, with two or three clean aprons and rubbers, and follow the rules laid down in the easy method prescribed in the following receipts; and if it is not the most egregious blunderer in the world I'll be answerable for all that is done amiss. What my friend Clouet will say when he hears of this rash adventure of mine I cannot guess; but this I'm sure of, he'll be my voucher that it is all authentic.

As to the character of that gentleman, much at this time must not be said: that he was an honest man I verily believe, and might I have leave to give him praise equal to his merit, I would venture to say he was worthy of the place he enjoyed in that noble family he had the honour to live in. Much has been said of his extravagance, but I beg pardon for saying it, he was not that at all, nay, so far from it, this I can aver, that setting aside the two soups, fish, and about five *gros entrees* (as the French call them) he has, with the help of a couple of rabbits or chickens, and six pigeons, completed a table of twenty-one dishes at a course, with such things as used to serve only for garnish round a lump of great heavy dishes before he came here, such as calves and lambs' sweetbreads, sheep and lambs' rumps, turkeys' livers, and many other such like things, of which, with proper sauces, he used to make as many pretty neat dishes. The second or third great dinner he drest for my Lord Duke, he ordered five calves' heads to be brought in, which made us think some extravagant thing was on foot, but we soon saw it was just the reverse of it; he made five very handsome and good dishes of what he took, and the heads not worth a groat less each. The tongues, pallets, eyes, brains, and ears. The story of his *affiette* of popes-eyes, the quintessence of a ham for sauce, and the gravy of twenty-two partridges for sauce for a brace, was always beyond the credit of any sensible person; so shall leave that untouch'd. The second course dishes, or *extremes*, he made as much difference in, I mean as to the expence, for what formerly (and that since my time too) made but one of most of them, he made two, and all prettier, because they were not so heavy. But I am afraid I shall launch out too far in encomiums on my friend Clouet; but beg to be excused by all my readers. One thing more and then I'll leave him to his new master marshal Richlieu (for there I am informed he now lives as steward, or *maitre d'hotel*). That I thought him very honest I think I said before, not only that, but he was of a temper so affable and agreeable, as to make every body happy about him. He would converse about indifferent matters with me or his kitchen boy, and the next moment, by a sweet turn in his discourse, give pleasure by his good behaviour and genteel deportment, to the first steward in the family. His conversation is always modest enough; and having read a little he never wanted something to say, let the topick be what it would.

POTAGES OR SOUPS

POTAGES OR SOUPS

Before we begin with Mr. Clouet's method or art of making his potages or soups, 'tis necessary first of all to point out his manner of preparing his bouillion or broth. Instead of the leg or shin of beef (which are the common pieces in your two-penny cut shops) take eight or ten pounds of the lean part, which, in London, is called the mouse-buttock, with a little knuckle of veal, neatly trimm'd, that it may serve to send up in your soup. A pot that holds three or four gallons will do. When you have wash'd your meat put it over the stove full of water; take care that 'tis well skimmed before it boils, or you'll lose the whole beauty of your soups and sauces; sprinkle in a little salt now and then, and 'twill cause the skim to rise; let it but just boil upon the stove, but take it off, and to simmer sideways, then all the soil will sink to the bottom; to season it take ten or twelve large sound onions, eight or ten whole carrots, three or four turnips, a parsnip, two or three leeks, and a little bundle of celery tied up, a few cloves, a blade or two of mace, and some whole white pepper; let it boil no longer than the meat is thoroughly boiled to eat; for to boil it to rags (as is the common practice) it makes the broth thick and grouty, and spoils the pleasing aspect of all your dinner, and hurts the meat that thousands of families would leap mast-high at; strain it through a lawn sieve into a clean earthen pan, skim the fat all off, and make your soups and gravies, &c., of it as you have directions in the following receipts.

N.B. Mons. Clouet never made use of either thyme, marjoram, or savoury in any of his soups or sauces, except in some few made dishes, as you'll see in going on; and where carrots are used be sure to cut off the rind, or 'twill give a reddish hue, which is disagreeable in any thing. This recipe of making my broth takes up a pretty deal of room; but as all the rest depends upon this being well done, 'tis of the utmost consequence to see that 'tis so. You may wonder of what use so many roots, &c., can be of; my answer is, you can make no savoury dish good without them. In this the French always were too cunning for us. The best of them all will not pretend to do any thing for the best gentleman in the kingdom, unless they could be allowed plenty of every thing from the garden. No, no. *Point des lesgumes; point de Cuisiniere.* No good garden things, no French cook. And from my own experience I know it to be so. I would venture myself to make a better soup with two pounds of meat, and such garden things as I liked, than is made of eight pound for the tables of most of our gentry, and all for want of better knowing the uses of roots and other vegetables. And now, my good cook, take care that this is well done; 'tis by this as 'tis by your *Aqua Fontana* in an apothecary's shop, scarce any thing can be done and finished well without it. After this I shall endeavour to be much more concise. I shall say nothing of drawing and trussing of fowls, and singing, peeling, scraping, picking, or washing of garden things, trimming of your meats, scaling or cleaning of fish, or any thing of that sort, for so much tautology would fill up a volume half as big as what I propose this to be, but shall put down the composition in as few words as it will admit of.—Next then—

TO MAKE A CLEAR GRAVY OF VEAL FOR SOUP

Three or four pound of a leg of veal, a slice of raw ham, in the middle of a stewpan, with a morsel of fat bacon under it, two or three onions, carrots, and some parsley upon it, pour in two or three spoonfuls of your broth, cover it close, set it upon a slow fire till it becomes dry and brown; but you must observe that that part of the pan that is uncovered with meat will take colour first, so that you must often move it round, that it may every part be of an equal brownness; and if you nick the time between its being of a nice brown and burning, put in your broth—full as many quarts as there is pounds of meat, let it simmer for half an hour or a little more, strain it through a lawn sieve; and if you have taken care you will find it of a fine colour, and clear as rock-water, and may use of it for any sort of gravy-soup or sauce.

SOUP SANTE OF CLEAR GRAVY

Potaget de Santé au jue clere

This soup is nothing more than a mixture of the broth and gravy in the foregoing receipts, putting them together either of a pale or deep brown, which is best approved on; prepare some crusts of two or three manchets, or French rowls, in a stewpan, boiling them till very tender in as much as will fill your soup-dish. You may boil your knuckle of veal in it if you have made a reserve of it, or a chicken, and serve it up boiling hot, and garnish your dish with some carrot, cut very thin and even, folded round one slice upon another; for all soups look neatest with a pretty garniture.

N.B. In such a soup as this the French frequently put a few pats of forcemeat fry'd nice and brown, and call it *Potage a la farce*. The manner of making it you'll find in one of the following receipts.

SOUP SANTE WITH HERBS

Potage de santé aux herbes

Of herbs or vegetables you must shift with celery and endives in the winter, but add a lettuce if you can get it; provide a duckling, or a chicken neatly blanch't, and boil it in your soup, which is nothing more than the same broth and gravy as before. With the celery, &c., cut in bits about an inch long; let it boil gently for an hour or so, and when 'tis almost your time of dining add a little spinage, sorrel, and chervil, chopt but not small, and boil it about five minutes; prepare your crusts as before in a stewpan, and lay at the bottom of your dish, lay your duckling in the middle, and pour your soup over it, and serve it up with some thin bits of celery for garnish, or without, as you like best.

For the summer season you may add a handful of young pease, heads of asparagus or sparagrass, nice little firm bits of cauliflower, bottoms of artichokes, and many other things that the season affords; 'tis but altering the name from one to the other, as you make your bills of fare daily; and you make twenty soups by this one receipt as easy as one; for instance, *Soup sante aux petit pois*, i.e. with young pease; so on to the rest.

SOUP A LA JULIENNE

Potage

This is a favourite soup, and now highly in vogue, and not much more expensive than the former. Instead of beef and veal for its broth, make it of a hen and veal and a bit of ham, seasoned as before. Make your gravy of it as for *Soup sante*; provide some bits of carrots about an inch in length, cut longways, slice it very thin, and cut it into small square pieces the full length; prepare some turnips in the same manner, some celery in the smallest bits you can of equal length; blanch all this two or three minutes, strain them, and put them in your soup-pot, and when your gravy is ready strain it to them; add to this a little purslane, the hearts of two or three lettuce, a little chervil, spinage, and sorrel, minced fine, and boil it together gently for an hour; get your crusts ready as before, and serve it up. If green pease are to be had fling in a handful or two, but very young, for old ones will thicken your soup, and make it have a bad look. You may serve a chicken up in it, or veal as before.

QUEEN'S SOUP, WHAT QUEEN I KNOW NOT

Potage a la reine

To make a proper stock for this, to about three quarts of broth put about a pound of lean veal and some bits of ham, two or three whole onions, carrots, parsley, and a blade of mace; boil it all together as you do gravy, for an hour; take all from your broth, and stir in the white part of a roasted fowl or chicken, and about two ounces of sweet almonds blanch'd, and both well pounded, the yolks of three or four hard eggs mash'd, with the soft of a manchet boiled in good milk or cream; rub it well through an etamine, and pour it into your soup-pot; take care to keep it boiling hot, but never let it boil a moment over your stove, but keep it moving; provide some crusts well soak'd, and a chicken in your dish, and serve it up, with a little of your best gravy poured in circles or patches. This is the most modern way.

Another fashion I have often seen, and I think no bad one where plate is used: put your soak'd bread into your dish, and set on a chaffing-dish of charcoal so that it boil to cleave to the bottom; but take care you don't let it burn: and yet it ought to be pretty brown, and should be scraped off with the soup-spoon. No other difference but that.

NANTILE SOUP

Potage aux nantiles

Nantiles are a sort of grain that come from abroad, and are sold at most of the oil-shops in London, in shape like a vetch or tare, but much less. Take about a quart of them, and boil in water only till very tender, for your stock. You must be so extravagant as to have a roasted partridge; pick off the flesh, and I'll presently shew the use of it: the bones you may crush to pieces, and put to them some bits of ham, with about three quarts of broth and gravy mix'd: add to it as before onions and carrots and parsley; boil this as the last; take all from it; see that your partridge meat is well pounded, and your nantiles, and stir them into your broth, and let boil a few minutes; strain it through your etamine, and serve it with a partridge in the middle, and some thin morsels of bacon for garnish, which may be both boil'd in your broth, being well blanch'd; have some crusts soak'd as before, and serve it up.

PEASE SOUP

Potage a la purée verte

If you make this soup in the season of green-pease, take about three pints of old ones, boil them tender, and pound 'em well, a bit of butter in a large stewpan, and fry, with some bits of ham, two or three carrots, onions, turnips, and a parsnip, a leek or two, some bits of celery, and mint-tops, a little spice and whole pepper; pour in about three quarts of broth, and boil it an hour; take all out, and put in your pease, with the soft of a French roll well soak'd in a little broth, for pease will not thicken enough at this time of the year; set it over your fire a few minutes, and pass it through your etamine; provide a little celery and endives, or lettuce ready boiled, with a few young pease; put them to your soup, and let it simmer till dinner-time; add a little handful of spinage and sorrel chop'd, which may boil five minutes; prepare your crusts as before, and serve it up with a square bit of bacon cut in bits through the rind, and may be boiled with your broth.

For the winter season make use of blue pease, which are always to be had in London, and celery and endives to serve up in it; and stain it with the juice of spinage.

RICE SOUP

Potage au ris

Get about a pound of rice, wash and pick it very clean; boil it a little while in water only; strain it thro' a sieve, and put it into your soup-pot; put as much broth to it as may boil it without danger of burning; put in a blade of mace, and keep it stirr'd; when 'tis quite soft you may serve it up with some of your best gravy poured round (as in the *Soup a la reine*).

Potage au Vermicelle; or VERMICELLI SOUP, is done just after the same manner; so needs no other receipt.

ONION SOUP

Potage aux onions

It differs from a clear gravy before prescribed only in this; take three or four large onions, take off the second coat, and slice them in halves very thin, lay them in water a while, dry them, and fry them of a nice brown, in a bit of fresh butter, pour in a little warm water, and strain 'em upon a sieve that they may not be greasy; put them into your soup to boil a few minutes; order your crusts as before, put to the bottom of your dish; pour your soup in, and serve it up with a knuckle of veal or without as you like best. Very small onions are sometimes used for a change; fry'd in the same manner, whole.

CRAWFISH SOUP

Potage aux ecrevisses

You make this soup with the broth of meat or fish, just as you like best; for your stock you must provide two or three small flounders, eels, gudgeons, &c., put 'em boiling in about three quarts of broth or cold water; when it is pretty nigh upon boiling be sure you skim it well. If you chuse the maigre sort, put in half a dozen onions, three or four carrots cut in pieces, and some parsley, a little spice and whole pepper, about three-quarters of a hundred of crawfish if pretty large will do; take off the small claws and the shells of the tails, and pound them fine, and boil 'em with your stock, about an hour, strain it off, and break in some crusts of French bread to thicken it, and if you can the spawn of a lobster, (that within gives the best colour), pound it, and put to it, strain it through your etamine, and keep it boiling hot only. My reason for it, is this: when it boils, if 'tis two minutes, all the beauty of it (which is the colour) subsides, and the broth swimming at top, put your crawfish in, make hot, only preserve a few to lay round your dish, with a rim of small flips of bread fastened with the white of an egg to prevent their rolling in. No bread with this soup.

Prawns make an excellent soup done just in the same manner; but you must observe there is a small bag in the carcass full of gravel, which must be always taken out before you pound them for your stock. You take only the tail of the prawn to put into your soup; but the crawfish body and all, but the small legs and shells.

This is a soup maigre you see; if broth is better liked put that.

HODGEPODGE OF BEEF WITH SAVOYS

Bouillis des tendrons de boeuf aux choux

Provide a piece of the middlemost part of brisket beef about six pound, cut it in square pieces so as to make ten or twelve of it; don't put it into too big a pot, but such a one as will be full with a gallon of water to it; take care to skim it well, and season it well with onions, carrots, turnips, leeks and celery, and a little bundle of parsley, and some pepper; when your meat is boiled very tender, strain your broth from it, and put it into a soup-pot or stewpan; take another with an ounce or little more of butter, melt it, and put in a large spoonful of flour, stir it over the fire till it becomes brown, take the fat off your broth and put to it, boil it a few minutes, and strain to your beef; your savoys should be well blanch'd, and tied up separate, put them into your meat, and let it stew very gently till your dinner is called; take it off and clean all from the fat, place your meat in neat order in your dish or soup-dish, lay your savoys between, pour your soup or sauce over it, and serve it up with a little parsley sprinkled genteely over it. This dish is frequently sent to table with turnips or carrots instead of savoys, cut in neat bits, and boiled, before you put them to your soup.—'Tis but to say, *des tendrons aux carrots*, i.e. with carrots, or *aux navets* with turnips.

Hodgepodge of veal or mutton is done after the same manner, with this difference only, instead of making your soup brown stir your flour no longer than while it retains its whiteness, and pour your broth in, and strain to your meat.

SOUP FOR SUPPER

Un plat de soup pour souper

This may seem to be but a simple thing to place among these high matters; but I never see it come from table without a terrible wound in it. If it has but the approbation of few it will pay very well for the room it takes up here.

To a quart of good new milk put a pint of cream, a bit of lemon-peel, a laurel-leaf or two, and a stick of cinnamon, and a few coriander seeds, and some good sugar; boilt it for a few minutes, and set off to cool; blanch two ounces of sweet almonds, with two or three bitter ones, pound them with a drop of water to a paste, and stir them in your milk, rub it through an etamine, pour it back into your stewpan, and make it just boiling. Provide the yolks of about ten eggs, and pour in beat nice and smooth, stir it upon your stove carefully for a minute or two, and it is ready to serve to table, putting on it some rusks or toasts of French bread.

WATER SOUCHY

This is rather a Dutch dish, and for change no bad one. To make this in perfection you should have several sorts of small fish, flounders, gudgeons, eels, perch, and a pike or two; but it is often with perch only; they ought to be very fresh; take care all is very clean, for what they are boiled in is the soup; cut little notches in all, and put them a little while in fresh spring water; (this is what is called crimping of fish in London); put them into a stewpan with as much water as you think will fill your dish, half a pint of white wine, a spoonful or two of vinegar, and as much salt as you would for broth. Put them over your fire in cold water, and take particular care you skim it well in boiling; provide some parsley roots cut in slices, and boiled very tender, and a large quantity of leaves of parsley boiled nice and green. When your fish have boiled gently for a quarter of an hour take them from the fire, and put in your roots, and when you serve it to table strew your leaves over it; take care not to break your fish, and pour your liquor on softly and hot; some plates of bread and butter are generally served up with this, so be sure to have them ready.

HERB SOUP WITHOUT MEAT

Potage maigre aux herbes

For the summer season three or four carrots, a little bunch of green onions, a few beet-leaves, and a handful of spinage and sorrel, a little purslane and chervil, and two or three lettuce, and some spice and pepper, strip all into small bits and fry them in a large stewpan, with a bit of fresh butter; pour in about two quarts of water, and let it boil gently for an hour at least, strain it off to the soft of a French roll well soaked, and pass it through your etamine; prepare the heart of two of nice light savoys or cabbage, a couple of lettuce, and a handful or two of young pease, stew them well, and drain them upon a sieve; when it draws towards your dinner-time have ready the yolks of half a dozen eggs, mixed well with half a pint of cream; put your pease, &c., into the soup, and boil it for a few minutes, a few slices of white bread, then your cream and eggs; stir it well together, cover it down very close till you are ready for it, just shew it to the fire and send it up. This soup is frequently done with cucumbers quartered, and the seed cut out, instead of the things before-mentioned. For the winter, celery and endives, white beet-roots, sliced thin, or the bottoms of artichokes, which in some families are preserved for such uses, and in most of the oil-shops in and about London.

PEASE SOUP WITHOUT MEAT

Potage maigre aux pois

For this soup a great quantity of garden things is used, five or six large onions, as many carrots, and a turnip or two, three or four leeks, celery, plenty of spinage, sorrel, parsley and mint; cut and slice all these into a large stewpan, and fry as before, pour in about three quarts of water, (for some will be lost amongst so many roots and herbs), and boil about an hour and a half very softly, strain into a pan with some soft bread, and pass it through your etamine; prepare some blue or white pease, which is best liked or handiest, well pounded, and stir it from the lumps and strain it again, rubbing the pease well thro'; have some celery and endive, well boiled, a little spinage and sorrel cut and boiled with your soup; provide some white bread fry'd in small dice in a bit of good butter; strew it in your soup when it is dished up, and serve it to table.

Take care it don't burn, for it is very apt to do so when your pease are to it, so keep it stirring.

Potage aux Nantiles is done in the same manner, and common soups among foreigners throughout the winter; and I hope my friends of my own country will approve of them too.

FISH

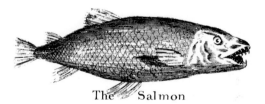

The   Salmon

FISH

Fish being the second first course dish takes its place next. N.B. Mr. Clouet never boiled any fish of any sort in the plain way; and as almost every body knows the easy method of dressing of them so, and their proper sauces, 'twill be needless to put it down here. I propose but four for his *gros entrées*, or removes, which is a turbot, salmon, a pike, and carps, done in manner following.

TURBOT IN THE ITALIAN WAY

Turbot a l'Italienne

Cut the fins and tail of your fish off, and lay to soak in a marinade for an hour or two, which is a little vinegar, white wine, salt and water, some green onions and bay leaves, with some blades of mace and whole pepper; take your fish and dry it upon a cloth, and place it in a stewpan just its size. The most common sauce in Mr. Clouet's way was that at top, *sauce Italienne*; to make which, with about a pint of good gravy, put a glass or two of Rhenish, two or three spoonfuls of oil, the juice of a couple of lemons, an anchovy or two, a little pepper and salt, some shallots minced very fine, and a little bundle of green onions and parsley tied up, pour it on your fish, so much as will just cover it; if you find this not quite enough add a spoonful or two of your *cullis, cover it down very close, and set it upon a slow stove to simmer very gently for about an hour, that it may be done rather by fumigation than hasty boiling; take a large ladle of your cullis and strain to it, about as much of your liquor from your fish, add a few olives pared from the kernel, or capers; dish your fish up hot, boil your sauce a few minutes and pour it over it, strewing a little parsley minced very fine over, and garnish with a great deal of whole, fresh and fine pick'd.

This is an excellent way to dress a John o'Dorey, or upon a pinch a large plaice is no bad thing.

SALMON WITH SHRIMP SAUCE

Saumon aux crevettes

Of a salmon the jowl is preferr'd to any other part; notch it to the bone on both sides about an inch apart; lay it in a marinade, as before mentioned; put it into some long stewpan just its bigness if you can, with a fish plate or napkin under it, that you may take it out without breaking; put to it a pint of white wine, a dash of vinegar, some sweet basil and thyme, whole pepper, salt and mace, two or three shallots, a bunch of parsley and green onions; pour in as much water as will just cover it, let your lid be shut close upon it, and about an hour before your dinner put it over a slow stove to simmer, and prepare your sauce as follows: provide as many small prawns or shrimps (the tails only) as you think necessary for your piece of salmon; put into your stewpan to them

*The next thing after these four of fish.

a proportionate quantity of cullis, add to it a little basil, pimpernel, thyme and parsley, all minced very fine, with a dash of white wine; boil all about a quarter of an hour, squeeze in the juice of a lemon or two, take care that the fish is well drained, and put meat into your dish, pour your sauce over, and serve it up; garnish with lemons cut in quarters.

Trouts may be done in the same manner.

At times when *maigre sauces* are chosen, make a little broth of a few small fish, season as above, skim it well, and boil it but about half an hour, strain it into a stewpan, add a bit of butter mix'd with some fine flour, provide the yolks of four or five eggs, and about a gill of cream; stir your butter, &c. to prevent its being lumpy, and let it boil a little while, set it off the fire, put in your prawns with your cream and eggs, cover it close for a few minutes, keep it moving over the stove for a moment, squeeze in your lemon, and serve it up.

Such a sauce as this may serve for any sort of fish, either stew'd or boil'd; and without the help of Mr. Clouet, I have many a time toss'd up a dish of fish with only its own natural broth seasoned in the manner prescribed; I mean by stewing and straining its broth, and thickened as above.

PIKE WITH FORCE-MEAT AND CAPER SAUCE

Un brochet farcez, sauce aux capers

Prepare your pike thus: gut it without cutting of it open, but take care it is well cleaned; cut a notch down the back from head to tail, turn it round, and fasten the tail in the mouth, and lay it in a marinade as before: for your farce or forcemeat take the udder of a leg of veal, or the kidney part of a loin of lamb, some fat bacon cut in dice, the spawn or melt of the fish, some green onions, a mushroom or two, or truffles, parsley, and salt, a little nutmeg and pepper, add a morsel of butter to fry it, chop it all well, and the soft of a French roll soak'd in cream or milk, pound all together in a large mortar, with three or four eggs; try if it is seasoned to your mind, and fill the belly of your fish, and close up that part that is cut in the back; make it nice and even; take two or three eggs, daub it well over, and strew some crumbs of bread upon it, and bake it in a gentle oven, the time according to the bigness of your pike. For your sauce, to two or three ladles of your cullis add two or three large spoonfuls of whole capers, some parsley minced fine, the juice of two lemons, a little minced shallot, and serve it up in your dish hot, but not poured over.

As this dish is bak'd, garnish with a large quantity of fry'd parsley.

The French are fond of barbel, chubs, or chevins, done in the same manner.

CARPS DONE THE COURT FASHION

Des carpes a la cour

A brace of carp is handsomest for a dish. Place your fish in a stewpan that they just fill, upon two or three slices of bacon or ham, that you may turn them the easier; pour in as much wine as will just cover them, a ladle or two of cullis, season with a bunch of onions and parsley, some cloves and mace, pepper, salt, and three or four bay leaves, and two or three shallots and mushrooms, an anchovy or two; and let your melts or soft rowes stew with the fish about half an hour; but the spawn or hard rowes boil separate, and when your sauce is ready cut it in pieces, and put in, for it is very apt to crumble to bits and spoil the comeliness of it. For the sauce take about half of what the fish are stewed in, and as much cullis added to it. For a *sauce hachée*, a little burnet, pimpernel, a mushroom or two, and some parsley, all minced very fine; take your melts or spawns and cut in small pieces, and boil a little while in your sauce; dish up your fish, add the juice of a lemon, and pour hot upon 'em; garnish with parsley only.

Tench may be done just in the same manner.

GROS ENTRÉES

The Sheep

GROS ENTRÉES

I propose to put twelve *gros entrées* of meat; but first of all to shew Mr. Clouet's method of preparing his coulis or cullis.

Take a stewpan that will hold about four quarts, put a thin slice or two of bacon at the bottom, about two pound of veal, a piece of ham, three or four carrots, onions and parsley, with a head or two of celery, pour in about a pint of your broth, cover it close, and let it go gently on upon a slow stove for an hour; when it comes to be almost dry watch it narrowly, so as to bring it to a nice brown, fill it up with broth, and let it boil softly about half an hour; take about half a pound of fresh butter, melt it, three or four large spoonfuls of fine flour, and rub over a stove till it is a fine yellowish or light-brown colour, pour it into your gravy, and stir it well after boiling ten minutes or so; take your meat and roots out, and pass it through your etamine; take off the fat, and set it handy for such uses as you'll find in the following receipts. Be sure great care is taken of this, for on it the goodness and beauty of all the rest depends.

LOIN OF VEAL MARINADED, WITH A BROWN SAUCE

Longe de veau marinée, sauce brune

Your loin of veal should be put into the marinade the day before; take about two quarts of new milk, and put to it some green onions, a shallot or two, parsley, a little spice, whole pepper, salt, two or three bay leaves, and some coriander seed; put your veal in, and keep it well turned so as to soak it well, till it should be spitted next day, cover it with paper with butter rubb'd on it, and roast it gently till it is well done. I have known a cook baste with this marinade, but Mr. Clouet never, nor with any thing else. For your sauce, mix about a pint of your cullis thinned with a little gravy, mince two or three mushrooms and capers, a little parsley, and a shallot or two, pour it into your dish, adding the juice of a lemon, with the kidney undermost.

HAM WITH SPINAGE

Un jambon aux epinars

In this the French beat us again. You scarce see a ham go to table fit to eat in the English way. We serve it up generally not half soak'd, salt as brine, and almost as hard as a flint, and our sauce most times nothing more than a little greasy cabbage and melted butter, and sometimes for garnish an ugly fowl or two, or half a dozen pigeons badly trussed. The French go another way to work; they take their ham and trim every jot of the outside off (*et mettez le tremper*) put it in soak two or three days in milk and water, and with a handful of coriander seeds; and in boiling they throw in a little white wine, and a few blades of mace, and whole pepper, a carrot or two, and an onion, which adds to the flavour and but a trifling expence; let it simmer for four or five hours, or till it is tender as a chicken; take care to preserve it whole, and make your sauce thus; stew your spinage nice and green, squeeze the juice from it quite dry, and chop it fine, put to it in a stewpan a ladle of your cullis, a little pepper, salt and nutmeg, see that it is of a good flavour and thickness, and serve it up with the juice of a lemon under your ham, with the skin taken clean off.

ROASTED HAM

Jambon rotis

For this entrée is generally provided a new Westphalia or Bayonne ham, soaked as before; put it to a slowish fire, and baste it with a little Rhenish or other white wine pretty constantly till it is done; but before you spit it draw your knife round between the fat and the sward; and in roasting you may easily take it all off; make it of a nice colour, and for your sauce dash into it a ladle or two of your cullis, a glass of Champagne or Rhenish, and a few tops of asparagus, cauliflower, or capers, add the juice of a lemon, and serve it up hot.

JIGGOT OF MUTTON WITH SPANISH ONIONS

Jigot de mouton aux onions Espaniols

A jigot of mutton is the leg with part of the loin; provide such a one as has been killed two or three days at least, thump it well, and bind it with packthread, that you keep whole when you take it out; put it into a pot about its bigness, and pour in a little of your broth, and cover it with water; put in about a dozen of Spanish onions, with the rinds on, three or four carrots, a turnip or two, some parsley, and any other herbs you like; cover down close, and stew it gently for three or four hours; but take your onions after an hour's stewing, and take the first and second rinds off, put 'em into a stewpan, with a ladle or two of your cullis, a mushroom or two, or truffles minced, and a little parsley; take your mutton and drain clean from the fat and liquor; make your sauce hot, and well seasoned, squeeze in a lemon, and serve it up with the onions round it, and pour the sauce over it.

CHINE OF MUTTON WITH CUCUMBER SAUCE, OR A SAUCE OF HERBS MINCED

Chine de mouton aux concombres, ou sauce hachée

You must provide the two fore-quarters of mutton, small and fat; cut it down the sides, and chop thro' the shoulders and breasts, so that it may lay even in your dish, raise the skin all off without cutting or tearing; prepare *un petit salpicon des herbes*, as the French call it; i.e. scrape a little fat bacon, and take a little thyme, marjoram, savoury, parsley, three or four green onions, a mushroom or two, and a shallot, mince all very fine, and fry them gently in the bacon; add a little pepper, and when it is almost cold, with a paste-brush daub it all over the back of your meat, skewer the skin over it, spit it with three or four large skewers, and wrap some paper over it well buttered, roast it enough very gently, and for your sauce provide some cucumbers (if in season) nicely quarter'd and fry'd in a bit of butter to a brown colour; strain them upon a sieve for a minute or two, and put them into a ladle or two of your cullis, boil them a little while, and throw in some minced parsley, the juice of a lemon, and serve it up.— For your hachée, or sauce of herbs, prepare just such matters as are fry'd for the first part of it; take a stewpan, with as much of your cullis as is necessary, and strew all in, and boil about half an hour very softly; take the paper and skin of your chine, and send it to table with the sauce poured over it, adding the juice of a lemon; and taste it to try if it is well flavour'd.

The hind chine of mutton is not so commonly dressed among the French, but sometimes done in the same way.

HIND CHINE OF MUTTON AFTER THE FASHION OF MR. CLOUET

Chine dernière de mouton en surprize a la Clouet

Provide a nice small fat chine not too fresh; take off the skin as the other, make a sort of paste of butter, mixt with some thyme, parsley, and a mushroom, a little pepper and salt, smear it over the back, and fillets of your meat, and skewer on the skin, spit with skewers (for nothing is more disagreeable than a spit-hole through all the meat), roast it gently with some paper over it; but take care 'tis not too much done; for it is hash'd in the manner following; raise the skin so as to preserve it whole, and cut the fillets out from end to end, and those of the inside, and save all its gravy; keep your bones hot before the fire, and cut your fillets ten times thinner than a wafer if it's possible; put to it a ladle or two of your cullis, with the gravy, a shallot or two minced, and some minced parsley, toss it up over a stove till 'tis boiling hot, but don't boil it a minute, squeeze in a lemon, dish up your chine, pouring the hash over it, and cover it with the skin neatly, and send it up.

With a great deal of care a shoulder of mutton may be done in the same manner. These are dishes that never fail of being well eaten.

TWO HIND-QUARTERS OF LAMB, WITH SPINAGE

Rots boeuf, d'agneau, ou deux quartiers d'agneaux derriere, aux epinars a la creme

Take your two quarters of lamb, truss your knuckles in nicely, and lay it in soak two or three hours in some milk, coriander seed, a little salt, two or three onions and parsley; put it boiling in but little water, skim it well, put in some flour and water well mixt, a lemon or two pared and sliced, a bit of sewet, and a little bunch of onions and parsley, stir it well from the bottom, and boil it gently, and these ingredients will make it white as a curd; prepare your spinage as for the ham, with this difference, instead of cullis with that seasoning; put to it about a pint of cream, a bit of butter mixt with flour, a little pepper and salt and nutmeg, stir it over a slow stove till it is of a nice consistence, squeeze in the juice of a lemon, pour it into the dish, and lay your lamb upon it after draining it from fat and water, and take off any of your seasonings that may chance to hang to it.

A neck of veal is frequently done in the same way, taking the chine-bone off, and trimming it neatly.

SURLOIN OF BEEF, THE FILLET HASH'D

Surloin de boeuf, fillet hachée

Trim your beef to look decent, and put it into a marinade the day before, as you did your veal, wrap it up in paper to roast it; take out the inside fillet, and slice it very thin; take care of your gravy, and put your meat into a stewpan with it, and as much of your cullis as is necessary to well fill the part where the meat was taken out, with some flowing in the dish; season with only pepper, salt, a shallot or two, and minced parsley; make it thorough boiling hot; add the juice of a lemon, and serve it up what we call the wrong side uppermost.

TURKEY IN A BRAIZE WITH CHESNUTS, WITH A SALPICON SAUCE
Dindon a la braize aux chataignes, sauce salpicon

Lard your turkey with a few large square pieces of bacon, seasoned with a little beaten spices, pepper and salt, and a little parsley; take a pot about its bigness, and line it with thin slices of bacon, and cover with the same; season pretty high, with onions, carrots, a turnip or two, such herbs as you like, a little spice and pepper, parsley, and a head or two of celery, fill up with a little broth and water mixt, cover it down close, and let it go gently on till every part of your turkey is very tender.

N.B. This braize will serve for any thing else the same day, or for four or five days following. I should first have spoke of preparing the chesnuts by blanching, peeling, and putting into the body of the turkey, with a little farce or force-meat in the crop, and skewer'd up; let your turkey lay in the braize till towards dinnertime; and now prepare your salpicon; take a thin slice or two of boiled ham, a veal sweetbread, the yolk or two of hard eggs, or a knot is better, a pickled cucumber or two, two or three mushrooms cut all into small dice, and put into as much cullis as is suitable for your dish, dash in a glass of Champagne, or other white wine; boil all a little while, throw in a little minc'd parsley, try if it is seasoned to your mind, squeeze in the juice of a lemon, and pour over your turkey well drained, and serve it up.

A couple of large fowls done in the same manner serves very well for a large *entrée*, with the same sauce, only leave out the chesnuts.

PIECE OF BEEF TREMBLING

Piece du boeuf tremblant

A rump of beef is the best piece for this, but it must be vastly cut and trimm'd; cut the edge of the aich-bone off quite close to the meat, that it may lay flat in your dish, and if it is large cut it at the chump end so as to make it square, hang it up for three or four days or more without salt; prepare a marinade as before, and leave it all night in soak, fillet it two or three times across, and put it into a pot, the fat uppermost, put in as much water as will a little more than cover it, take care to skim it well, and season as you would for a good broth, adding about a pint of white wine; let it simmer for as long a time as it will hang together; there are many sauces for this piece of meat; but the two favourites with Clouet were *sauce aux carrots* and *sauce hachée*; sauce with carrots, and a sauce of herbs, &c. minced. Your carrots should be cut an inch long, and boiled a little in water, and afterwards stewed in some cullis proportionate to your meat; when they are done tender, dash in a glass of white wine, a little minced shallot and parsley, and the juice of a lemon; take your beef out upon a cloth, clean it neatly from its fat and liquor, place it hot and whole in your dish, and pour your sauce hot over it, and serve it up. The *sauce hachée* you saw before. But strew some minced parsley over it, it looks prettier.

A RAISED DUCKLING PYE

Pattée dressée des canards

Take the livers of your ducklings, and make a little forcemeat with a little scraped bacon, a mushroom or two, some herbs, pepper, salt and nutmeg pounded well together, a morsel of soft bread, and an egg or two, mix it well, and put it into them, put 'em into your crust with a bunch of onions and parsley, a little pepper strewed over, and cover them with some slices of bacon, and finish your making: before you send it to table, take a little broth and cullis mixt; take out your bacon and fat, and pour in your sauce, with the juice of a lemon and serve it up without the lid.—You may add the heads of a few asparagus, or green pease, in your sauce.

GOOSE-PYE LARDED WITH BACON

Pattée d'oison picquée

Provide a young fat goose, and lard in a few pieces of bacon, seasoned with spice, pepper and salt, and some herbs; place in your crust, and sprinkle a little salt and pepper, pour in a little broth, a bunch of onions and parsley, with a little shallot, and cover it with a slice or two of bacon; bake it well, and provide a sauce as follows: take the feet, pinions, and gizzard of your goose, stew them well, put them into a stewpan with a ladle of your cullis seasoned with such matters as you have seen before; cut up your pye and pour it in; but take off the fat clean, for nothing is more disagreeable in a sauce than the oily fat of a goose, turkey, or a fowl.

CALVES' HEADS WITH RAGOUT MELÉE

Tête de veau au ragout melée

To make this for a large or *gros entrée* you must provide two* heads, but you need take nothing more than the cheeks; the tongues, pallats, &c. you may put to some other uses; blanch your cheeks, after taking the bones out, tie them up together the skins outermost, with a morsel of bacon between, stew them with such seasoning as before, and prepare your *ragout melée* as follows: take a veal sweetbread or two, or three of lambs, some little square bits of bacon, two or three knots of eggs, a liver or two of fowls or turkey, some lambs or cocks stones cut into pieces, stew all a little while in a ladle of your cullis, a little parsley, pepper and salt, squeeze in the juice of a lemon, part your cheeks, and pour in your ragout between an equal quantity of each; preserve a little to pour over, and serve them up.

*One may do very well for a small dish

NEATS TONGUE ROASTED WITH RHENISH WINE, PIQUANT SAUCE

Langue de boeuf rotis au vin de Rhin, sauce piquante

For a large *entrée* you ought to provide two tongues, lay them fresh into a marinade some hours, spit 'em, and cover them with paper buttered, and baste them well and often with some Rhenish wine mixt with as much well seasoned broth; for your *sauce piquante* get a parcel of herbs, such as tarrogan, pimpernel, thyme, basil, parsley, and some shallots minc'd very fine; boil all in a glass or two of Champagne or Rhenish a few minutes, with a little pepper and salt, and pounded mace; take a large ladle of your cullis, squeeze in the juice of two or three lemons or oranges; when your tongues are done tear off the skins, and dish them up nice and hot, and pour your sauce over them, and garnish with lemons and oranges in quarters.

PIECE OF BEEF OF A SCARLET COLOUR, WITH
A CABBAGE OR SAVOY SAUCE

Piece de boeuf a l'ecarlate, sauce aux choux

A square piece of the middle of the brisket is what is generally provided for this dish, about six or eight pound, take half a pound of salt-petre, beat it well, and rub over your beef, wrap it up in a cloth, and bury it in salt for seven or eight days, but not to touch the salt; stew it in the manner of *boeuf tremblant*, and season'd so; let it be done very tender, and your cabbage or savoy be blanch'd, tied up, and stew'd with it for an hour, squeeze the fat and liquor well from 'em, and put them into a stewpan with a ladle or two of cullis; add a little challot, minced parsley, and the juice of a lemon; take out your beef upon a cloth to drain it well, dish up with your cabbage round it, cut it in notches across, and pour your sauce over it very hot.

This is sometimes served to table with lettuce, tops of asparagus, carrots, turnips, or any sort of garden things the sauces are made of.

LEG OF VEAL MARINADED WITH SAUCE OF ENDIVES

Cuisse de veau marine, sauce a la chicoree

Provide a nice leg of white veal, and marinade it in the manner of your loin, roast it with some lards or slices of bacon over it, covered with paper, take four or five heads of endives cut into bits about an inch in length, blanch it a little, and stew it in a little gravy mixt with a ladle of cullis; put a minced shallot and some parsley, squeeze in the juice of a lemon, and serve it up with the sauce under it.—Make use of capers, olives, or any sort of pickles for a change.

PETITS ENTRÉES

Pheasant.

PETITS ENTRÉES

The next twenty are what the French call *petits entrées*.—Dishes of a lesser size.

Four of fish, four of meats, four of pastry, four of fowls, and four others.

MATELOTTE OF CARPS

Matelotte des carps

Provide one large, or a brace of a smaller size, cut in seven or eight pieces, fry them in a bit of fresh butter, pour in about a pint of red wine, a ladle of gravy, tie up a bunch of green onions, herbs and parsley, a few cloves, pepper and salt, and three or four bay leaves, stew all together gently about three quarters of an hour, strain it into another stewpan to as much cullis as will do for your dish, and put your fish to it, put your bay leaves in, and a spoonful or two of capers, an anchovy chopt very fine; add the juice of a lemon and serve it up, with your melts or spawn for garnish, boiled in a little vinegar, salt and water; and have some bits of bread fry'd to stick about between your pieces of fish.

Tench and eels make an excellent dish done the same way.

FRICASEE OF EELS WITH CHAMPAGNE, OR RHENISH WINE

Fricasee des anguilles au vin de Champagne,
ou vin de Rhin

Skin three or four large eels, and notch them from end to end, cut 'em into four or five pieces each, and lay them from end to end, and lay them in some spring water for half an hour to crimp them, dry them in a cloth, and toss them over a fire a few minutes in a bit of fresh butter, a green onion or two, and a little parsley; but take care the colour of neither is alter'd by burning your butter; pour in about a pint of white wine, and as much good broth, pepper, salt, and a blade of mace; let it stew about as long as the carp above, and thicken it with a bit of butter and flour, prepare your *liaison* (as the French call it) with the yolks of four or five eggs beat smooth, with two or three spoonfuls of broth, grate in a little nutmeg, a little minced parsley; towards your dinner-time let your eels be boiling hot, and pour in your egg, &c., toss it over the fire for a moment, add the juice of a lemon, and serve it up. Be very cautious you don't let it curdle by keeping it too long upon the fire after the eggs are in, for if 'tis ever so good and palatable before, nobody at table will touch it, from its bad appearance.

Tench cut in pieces make a very good dish done as above.

SOLES WITH FORCEMEAT, SAUCE OF MINCED HERBS

Des soles farcéz, sauce aux fines herbes

For this provide a pair of large soles, or three or four of a lesser size, take the skin off from both sides, and soak them in a marinade, as shewn before, for an hour, dry them upon a cloth, cut them down the middle, and with the point of your knife raise up the fillets; make a little forcemeat of the flesh of a couple of plaice or flounders, a morsel of the fat of veals udder or sewet, season with a mushroom or two, a green onion and parsley minced, pepper and salt and nutmeg, scrape a bit of bacon, and fry it very gently; let it cool, and pound it well with a bit of bread well soak'd and couple of eggs, taking away one white; lift up the flesh of the soles, and crowd in as much as you can; brush some egg over them, and strew crumbs of bread, a litle oil, or oil'd butter poured upon it; bake 'em about half an hour of a fine colour, and send them up garnished with some little pats of your forcemeat fry'd, and some parlsey. For your sauce take a little sweet basil, pimpernel, thyme and parsley, a shallot or two minced fine, with a ladle of your clear gravy, and a dash of white wine, pepper and salt; boil all together for a few minutes, squeeze in a lemon or two, and send it up in a fish sauce-boat.

Small prills are good done in this manner, or any other firm-flesh'd fish.

SALMON IN SLICES MR. CLOUET'S FASHION, WITH CRAWFISH SAUCE, OR PRAWNS

Des tranches de saumon a la Clouet, sauce des ecrevisses ou des crevettes

Take about six slices of salmon, and lay in soak in what the French call a hot marinade; scrape some fat bacon, or a piece of butter, and a little minced shallot, a green onion, a mushroom, sweet basil and parsley, and a very little pepper and salt; fry all gently for two or three minutes, and put your salmon immediately in it, and keep it turn'd pretty often, with a few slices of lemon and a bay leaf or two; lay it upon your grid-iron made very hot, that you may turn it well; prepare a little cullis of prawns or crawfish. As for the crawfish soup, stew the tails in it a quarter of an hour, with an anchovy chopt fine; add the juice of a lemon, dish up your fish with the sauce pour'd over, and garnish with either of your shell-fish, taking the shell from the tail.

Trouts make an exceeding good dish after the same manner, only broiled whole, and cut in little notches from eye to fork.

A CHICKEN PYE WITH LIGHT CRUST

Un pattée de poulets aux feuilletages

Cover the bottom of your dish or pattypan with a nice light paste, cut your chickens as for a fricasee, lay them in, and season with pepper, salt, and a bit of mace, put in a little bundle of green onions and parsley tied, a spoonful or two of broth, cover with thin slices of bacon; put your lid nicely on, and bake it about an hour and an half; before you serve it up take off the top, your bacon out, and clean well from fat; have ready a ladle of cullis, with the heads of a few asparagus, or pease, or anything thing else that is in season; make it boiling hot, with the juice of a lemon, and serve it up.

Young rabbits make a good pye in the same way.

PARTRIDGE PYE WITH ENDIVES

Pattée des perdreaux a la chicorée

Cut off the pinions of your birds as for roasting, the feet to the knee-joint, tuck the thighs in, and lard them with about six bits of bacon each side, make a little forcemeat of the livers, a little scrap'd bacon, a green onion and parsley, and a mushroom minced fine, and put withinside, lay bottom crust, and your birds in, with pepper, salt, &c., as before, and cover with bacon; fix on your lid, and bake it about two hours; provide some endive cut pretty small, and boil it very tender in a little broth, pour a ladle of cullis, some pepper and salt, and a morsel of shallot; cut up your pye clear of the fat and bacon, boil your sauce a little while, squeeze in the juice of orange and lemon, pour it over your partridges, and serve it up.

PIGEON PYE WITH SPINAGE

Pattée des pigeoneaux aux epinars

Take about eight small wild pigeons, or as many large squab pigeons, which are best in season, take the livers and make a forcemeat as before, and put it into them, season as the last, cover with bacon, lay them in your paste, and cover them; bake it about an hour and an half, and provide your spinage stew'd nice and green, squeeze the juice well from it, chop it well, put it into a stewpan with a ladle of cullis, a little pepper, salt and nutmeg; let it stew for a few minutes, squeeze in the juice of a lemon; get your pye ready as directed before, and pour it in, and send it up very hot.

PETTY-PATTIES OF VEAL SWEETBREADS

Des petits pattés aux ris de veau

For this dish take six small tartpans, if you have nothing for the making such things in, and lay your paste in, provide a couple of sweetbreads, boil them ten minutes or a quarter of an hour, and put 'em into cold water to harden a little, take three or four slices of ham, a mushroom or two, cut all into small dice, and fry in a little scraped bacon with a green onion or two, a little parsley, pepper, salt and nutmeg, get the yolks of three or four hard eggs, and a pickled cucumber or two, and cut to the rest when fry'd a little while very softly; stir all together, and put it into your paste, with a spoonful of gravy, bake them in a brisk oven about half an hour, cut off the lids, and set 'em in your dish, take a ladle of cullis, with a little gravy, a little chop'd parsley, make it boiling hot, with the juice of orange or lemon, pour it into your patties, put on the lids and serve them up.

You may make such a sort of a dish as this almost at any time, with what your house affords, such as the breast of a fowl or chicken, with a slice or two of tongue, a partridge or woodcock, or the like.

N.B. There is a favourite sauce now in high vogue called *a la Benjamelo*; that is as often served with these little matters which shall be given in some of the following receipts.

FILLET OF MUTTON WITH CUCUMBERS OR CELERY

Fillet de mouton aux concombres ou celery

Provide one large or two small necks of mutton, cut off a good deal of the scrag, and the chine and splaybones close to the ribs, tear off the fat of the great end, and flat it with your cleaver, that it may lay neat in your dish, soak it in a marinade as before, and roast wrapt up in paper well buttered; for your sauce in the spring or summer, quarter some cucumbers nicely, and fry them in a bit of butter, after laying in the same marinade, stew 'em in a ladle or two of your cullis, a morsel of shallot or green onion, pepper and salt, a little minced parsley, the juice of a lemon, and serve it. The only difference between this and the celery sauce is, instead of frying your celery, boil it very tender in a little water, or broth if you have plenty, and stew it for a quarter of an hour; be cautious you don't break the cucumbers.

NECK OF VEAL WITH ENDIVE SAUCE

Caret de veau a la chicorée

Provide a nice white neck of veal, cut off the scrag, &c., as from the mutton, lay it to soak in such a marinade as for your loin of veal an hour or two, roast it with lards, or slices of bacon, to preserve its whiteness, and send it to table, the sauce under or upon it, which you like best, made just in the same manner as the celery sauce; but for either of these things, in the season, you may use pease, tops of asparagus, kidney beans, bits of artichoke bottoms or cauliflower; and if care is taken they are pretty dishes.

A RIB OF BEEF GLASSE WITH SPINAGE

Cote de boeuf glassée aux epinars

Provide one of the prime ribs, trim it neatly, and lay it in a marinade for an hour or two; take a stewpan exactly its bigness, put a slice or two of bacon at the bottom, lay in your beef, and cover it with the same; to season put in an onion or two, some bits of carrot, a little sweet basil, thyme and parsley, a little pepper, salt, and a blade or two of mace; let it stew gently till it is very tender; take it out upon a plate, strain your braize, clean it well from the fat, put it into a clean stewpan, and boil it with a ladle of gravy very fast, and you'll find it come to a sort of a gluey consistence, then put your beef in, and keep it hot till your dinner-time, and serve it up with spinage done in the same manner as that for the ham.

At another time you may serve it with savoys or red cabbage stript fine and stewed, after being blanch'd, only adding a bit of bacon, with a few cloves stuck in it in the stewing, but not to send to table.

Fillet de boeuf, or fillet of the surloin is done pretty much in the same way, marinaded and roasted, with bacon over it, and the same sort of sauces.

HARICOTS OF MUTTON WITH CARROTS

Haricot de mouton aux carrots

The old fashioned way of doing this dish, in my opinion, is a very bad one, and not only so but a very expensive one. Two or three fat breasts I have seen provided, cut into pieces ugly enough, and stewed three or four hours, in what I called before, a braize: a sauce is prepared for it, and the mutton again stewed in it, and as much fat sent to table as sauce. For this large dish I would advise the cook to take the best ends of two necks, take two bones to a cutlet, cut one off, and flat it well (I mean the cutlet), tear off the fat from the three or four bones of the prime end, trim them nearly, and fry 'em a few minutes over a brisk stove; for your sauce take the scrags and make a gravy, season in the same way as for that in the second receipt; make a cullis of it with a little flour stirred over the fire with a morsel of butter, pour it to your mutton, and stew it till it is tender; cut your carrots, boil them in water for a while, and put them to it, with some pepper, salt, and a bit of shallot; when dinner-time throw in some minced parsley, squeeze in some lemon-juice, lay your cutlets in the dish, and serve it up.

This is frequently done with small onions fry'd brown, or turnips cut in little square or round bits.

PHEASANT A LA MONGELAS WITH FAT LIVERS

Faisant a la mongelas aux fois gras

Provide a large pheasant, cut off the pinions as to roast, and with the liver make such a forcemeat as you have seen set down before, put it into your pheasant, and spit it, with some lards of bacon and paper, take care you roast it nicely, and prepare your sauce as follows; take some fat livers of turkeys or fowls, blanch them till thoroughly done, and pound 'em to a paste, put to some gravy and cullis, mix it well together, and pass it through an etamine; cut off the flesh of the pheasant, slice it very thin and put to it, and preserve the carcass hot; add to your sauce, which should be about the thickness of your cullis, a little pepper, salt, some minced parsley, and the juice of two or three oranges; and if you approve on't you may strip a few morsels of the orange-peel in, and serve it up with the hash poured over the breast, and garnish with some oranges in quarters.

A CAPON OR TWO POULETS, WITH A RAGOUT MELLEZ

Un chapon ou deux poulardes, sauce ragout mellez

Take a large capon or two poulets, and blanch nicely in a morsel of butter or scraped bacon, but cut off your pinions and feet, and tuck in the legs: prepare your ragout in manner following; get a sweetbread of veal, or two of lambs, the fat livers of a turkey or fowls, some cocks stones, three or four mushrooms, a thin slice or two of lemon, blanch all well with a knot or two of eggs, cut all into very small dice, and stew in a ladle of cullis; and you may add to it three or four gizzards and a few cocks combs boiled very tender; fill up the bellies of your fowls or capons, and sew up at both ends, but make a reserve of some of your ragout to pour over; put 'em upon a lark-spit across, and tie upon another, lard them with bacon, cover with paper, and roast them softly, that they may be nice and white, strew in a little minced parsley, a morsel of shallot, squeeze in the juice of a lemon or orange, and serve up with the ragout under.—Remember to draw the threads out.

PARTRIDGES, WITH CELERY SAUCE WHITE

Des perdreaux au celery blanc

Take three partridges, and make a forcemeat of the livers as before named, and put it into 'em, blanch 'em in a hot marinade, spit them across, and tie them upon another, put on some lards of bacon and paper, and roast them softly; for your sauce, take the hearts or white of six or eight heads of celery split two or three times, and cut to pieces about an inch long, blanch it a minute or two in water, then boil it in some good broth for an hour, put in a bit of butter mixt with flour to thicken it; prepare a liaison, or four or five yolks of eggs and some cream, a little pepper, salt, nutmeg and minced parsley, pour it to your sauce boiling hot, move it for a moment over your stove, squeeze in the juice of a lemon or orange, draw off your partridges, and dish them up with your sauce neatly over them.—This is an excellent sauce for boiled partridges or chickens, done in the same way as above prescribed.

WOODCOCKS, WITH ORANGE SAUCE

Des becasses aux oranges

Two brace of cocks I think is not too much for a dish as is here proposed; draw them without cutting off the heads, preserve the ropes and livers for a forcemeat to put withinside, twist the feet back and truss 'em neatly with the beak thro' the thighs, and tie the feet upon the vent, spit them upon a lark-spit across upon another, spit and roast them with lards of bacon; when roasted dish 'em up, and cut a gash or two in the breast of each, squeeze upon them the juice of two or three oranges; your sauce must be a clear gravy with a morsel of shallot, pepper, and salt; under each cock put a nice toast well soak'd in a hot cullis, and serve them up.

Snipes make a neat dish this way; but I shall make a reserve of them for an *Hors d'oeuvres*.

A HARE STEWED

Un lievre en casserole

One seldom sees a hare drest by the English any other way but roasted, or boiled with onions, so that if a gentleman kills sixty or seventy brace in a season he has no variety, and always stands in his bill of fare, a hare; no more. In this we are beat again. One good way, I presume, is this; and afterwards in the *Hors d'oeuvres*, and *entre mots*, shall shew how evident it is. For this then, to proceed—Take a young hare (a leveret is another thing) and cut into ten pieces, the two legs, two wings or shoulders, the chine in four, and the stomach and skirts in two, don't blanch them, but skim your wine, &c., well; put it into your stewpan, with about three half-pints of Port wine, two or three onions, a carrot or two, some sweet basil, thyme and parsley, and a ladle of gravy, a little salt and pepper, a clove or two, and a bit of mace, and let it stew gently for two hours, take out your hare clean into another stewpan, and strain your sauce to it, adding a ladle of cullis, and if not thick enough put in a bit of butter and flour, and boil it a minute, and keep it hot till your dinner is ready, fling in a spoonful or two of capers, some minced parsley, and the juice of a lemon or orange, and serve it up with some fry'd bits of bread in the dish and round it.—I hope nothing is said disagreeable or in prejudice of our English and plain way of dressing a hare, for I think it best; but variety adds beauty to a table. I have seen salmon, turbot, soles, &c., frequently served to a gentleman's table in the same one-way till they have come back almost untouch'd, till the end of the seasons, another cook has come along, changed their dresses, and by adding some little matter, and not a jot has remained in the dish; but yet in my opinion not so good. It is in this as it is in dress or equipage, sometimes white pleases best, and sometimes red, and so on to all the colours you can name.

A MATELOTTE OF CHICKENS WITH MUSHROOMS

Une matelotte des petits poulet aux champignons

Cut your chickens as for a fricasee, the legs and wings, pinions, breast and back in two, blanch them in water for two or three minutes, put 'em into a stewpan, with a bit or two of ham, a ladle of gravy and cullis mixt, season with a bunch of onions and parsley, a little sweet basil, a morsel of shallot, pepper, salt, a blade of mace; stew all together gently for an hour.
N.B. This sauce may serve for several good uses; but for your matelotte prepare it with a ladle or two of your cullis, with a few nice button mushrooms, put in your chickens, and stew all together, with a little pepper, salt and nutmeg; add the juice of a lemon or orange, and serve it up. The reason of changing the sauce is, that your dish may have a decent appearance: your mushrooms would be broke, and your herbs, &c., by so long stewing be crumbled, and spoil the beauty of the most favourite dish of all.

This is often done with pease or tops of asparagus.

RABBITS COLLARED, WITH A SAUCE A L'IVERNOISE

Des roulades des lapreaux, sauce a l'ivernoise

Two couple of young rabbits for this dish I think is not too many: take care to take the bones out quite up to the wings or shoulders, but leave them on with the head; prepare a nice hot forcemeat of some bits of the rabbits that may be spared, a bit of veal or lamb fat, a little scrap'd bacon, a morsel of green onion, a mushroom, pepper, salt, and a little pasley, fry all together for a few minutes; put it into a mortar with some soft of a French roll soaked in cream of milk, a little nutmeg, pound all well together with the yolks of two or three eggs; spread your rabbits in a dish, and lay your forcemeat on, roll them up to the wings, and bind with a bit of packthread; stew them in a braize about an hour and an half, and prepare your sauce thus: 'Tis a sort of a *sauce hachée*, as you have seen before, only to this you cannot put too many sorts of strong herbs, such as tarragon, pimpernel, thyme, marjoram and savoury, a green onion or two, mushrooms, and a bit of shallot, all minc'd very fine and separate; to a ladle or two of gravy and cullis mixt, put in just as much of each as will make palatable in boiling a quarter of an hour with pepper, salt and nutmeg, and a spoonful or two of good oil, throw in a handful of capers, clean your rabbits well from grease, add the juice of a couple of lemons or oranges, and dish up, with your sauce over.

SMALL FAT PIG EN BALON. SAUCE IN RAVIGOTTE

Un petit cochon de lait en balon. Sauce en ravigotte

'Tis not a common thing to see a pig dressed among us any other way than roasted; but if variety can please I beg leave to send one to table in the following fashion: Cut your pig open from head to tail, but not touch the skin on the back, cut the head close off, and bone the rest, cut off the superfluous bits and make a forcemeat, as in the receipt before, spread it regular, and cut some long thin bits of ham, the yolks of two or three hard eggs, and a bit of green pickle, cover all in with the ends and skirts of the pig, and tie it up quite tight in a thin cloth, just cover it with water well seasoned with onions, carrots, leeks, herbs and parsley, salt, whole pepper, and a little spice; let all simmer together for about two hours; prepare the sauce with a ladle or two of cullis, take a little pimpernel, a few leaves of sage, a mushroom or two, and some parsley, mince all separate, and boil all for a quarter of an hour; put in a small spoonful of mustard, squeeze in the juice of lemons or oranges, take out your balon nice and whole wipe it with a clean cloth, and dish it up, pouring your sauce over it; don't let your sauce boil after the mustard is in, 'tis apt to make it bitter.—If the balon should open tuck in the skirts under, with a spoon or point of your knife, that it may go decent to table.

I must ask leave to add four more of these *petits entrées*, because they are dishes in high fashion, and very much admired.

FRICANDO OF VEAL GLASSÉE, WITH SPINAGE BROWN

Fricando de veau glassée, aux epinars brune

Take the inner part of a leg of veal, what the French call the Nut, take all the little skins off, flat it down, and lard it all over with very small bits of bacon, put a slice or two into a stewpan about its bigness, and lay it in, cover with a slice of bacon or two more, and season with two or three onions, carrots and parsley, just cover it with water and a ladle of gravy, put no salt because of the bacon; let it simmer for about a couple of hours; take your veal out, and preserve it hot; strain your gravy into another stewpan, clean it well from fat, and boil it over a brisk stove till it comes to a caromel; lay your *Fricando* in (the larding downwards) and cover it close, for you cannot set it a minute upon the fire; the caromel will burn; prepare your sauce aux epinars, sauce with cullis, &c., as for your ham; dish up with your spinage at the bottom, and pour the caromel upon it. Take care that the caromel is of a nice brown, and you cannot have a genteeler dish.

CHICKENS IN THE DUTCH WAY, WITH PARSLEY ROOTS, AND LEAVES OF DITTO

*Des petits poulets a l'Hollandoise, aux racines
and feuilles de persil*

Three large chickens will be enough; cut off the pinions, but not the feet, strip off the stockings (as they are called) by fire or boiling water, and tie them down upon the breasts; make a forcemeat with the livers, &c., as before named, put into them, blanch them nice and white over a clear stove, put them upon a lark spit, and tie them to another, with some lards of bacon, and plenty of butter'd paper; take care they are exactly coloured as you would roast a chicken in the English way, and provide your sauce as here set down; take some parsley roots that are not sticky, take off the rinds, cut them in thin slices, and lay them to soak in vinegar, salt and water, a green onion or two, and some parsley and shallot, with a blade of mace and whole pepper, for two or three hours; fry them very softly in a bit of butter, and wash afterwards in warm water; put them into some cullis, with a good dash of white wine of the sharp sort, boil it all together with a minced mushroom or two, or a green truffle, a little pepper, salt and nutmeg, have a good quantity of parsley leaves boiled nice and green, stir it into your roots just before it goes to table; clean your chickens from grease, and lay them in your dish, make your sauce boiling hot, add the juice of two or three lemons or oranges, and serve it up.

A CALF'S LIVER A LA BOURGEOISE

Un fois de veau a la bourgeoise

Get the liver of a fat white calf, and lard it with large slips of bacon seasoned with spices, pepper and salt, and plenty of herbs minced very fine, put it into a stewpan with a slice or two of bacon under it, cover it with cold water, and take care to skim it well, season with an onion or two, bits of carrots, a bunch of herbs and a shallot and mushroom; let it stew gently for three quarters of an hour, and provide this sauce for it:—To a ladle of cullis put a small glass of white wine, and a spoonful of vinegar, a little pepper, salt and nutmeg, and such herbs as you used with the bacon, with some mushrooms minced; stew the liver in this a few minutes, squeeze in the juice of orange or lemon, and serve it up.

Livers of house-lambs make a pretty dish the same way.

LOAF OF BEEF-COLLOPS

Un pain des escalopes be boeuf

Order a loaf of French bread the size of your dish roll'd flattish, take out the inside, and fry the crust in butter; take as much of the fillet of a surloin, or the tender part of a rump of beef as will do for your loaf, hash it raw very thin, oil a bit of butter, and fry it quick, season with only a morsel of onion and parsley minced; for the sauce take a large ladle or two of cullis, season with pepper, salt and nutmeg, a mushroom or two and shallots minced very fine; stew this a few minutes, and put in the hash; but don't let it boil a minute after; sprinkle in a little minced, squeeze the juice of a lemon or orange, pour it in and over your loaf, and serve it up.

The fillet of a neck of veal makes a genteel and good dish in a loaf; put a white sauce, such as has been shewn in several of the receipts.

Nothing has been said of garlick for any of the dishes past, nor shall I say more than this at all, that it is agreeable to the taste of foreigners no doubt; and was I to dress a dinner for only such, should always make use of it; but as my chief aim is to please my countrymen, I shall leave it entirely to their choice. I never saw Mr. Clouet use more in any thing than a morsel mash'd with the point of his knife, and stirred in. But I have seen many a good dish spoil'd by the cook's not knowing its proper use. It is to give a flavour, and not to put so much as to make it predominant to all other ingredients.

Teal

HORS D'OUVRES

HORS D'OUVRES

The next thirty dishes, or thereabouts, are what the French call *Hors d'ouvres*, dishes of a small size, that are generally placed round the outer parts of the table, for first course dishes.

PALLETS OF BEEF, WITH CHAMPAGNE OR RHENISH WINE

Des pallets de boeuf au vin de Champagne ou vin du Rhin

Two or three pallets is enough for a small dish, scrape them clean, and boil for an hour in water, put them into cold a while, and peel the skins off, stew them in a braize till very tender, drain well from the fat, and cut them into pieces as nigh as you can in length two inches, in width one, put them into a stewpan with a small ladle of cullis, a little pepper, salt, and a morsel of shallot, stew all a few minutes with a glass of either of the wines, throw in a little minced parsley, juice of a lemon or orange, and serve it up. This is often sent to table with some onions fry'd nice and brown.

SLICES OF FILLET OF BEEF, WITH CLEAR GRAVY AND ROCOMBOLE

Des tranches de fillet de boeuf, au jus clair et rocombole

A pound of meat is enough for this dish; cut it into bits about an inch thick, and flat it down with your knife or a light cleaver; it is better than slicing; make it very thin and jagg it with the back of your knife cross and cross, rub a large stewpan with butter, a little green onion and parsley minced, fry your beef briskly for two or three minutes, tossing it that it may be done on both sides, take it out into a small stewpan, and pour in a ladle of nice gravy, a little pepper, salt, a morsel of shallot and parsley, boil it but a moment; when dinner is ready squeeze in a lemon or orange, and send it to table.

The inside fillets of loins of mutton or pork is done in the same manner; and though they seem but trifling matters, yet if care is taken to make them very thin, and nicely fry'd, and not boiled too much afterwards, they are good and pretty dishes.

SHEEPS RUMPS A LA BRAIZE, WITH A SAUCE OF CAPERS

Des queues de mouton a la braize, sauce aux capres

Do your rumps down very tender in a braize, trim them nicely, cut all the ragged bits off, and place 'em in a stewpan, pour in a ladle of cullis, a spoonful of capers, a morsel of shallot and minced parsley; boil all a few minutes, take the fat clean off, add the juice of a lemon or orange, and serve it up.

Lambs rumps done in this way make a very neat dish, and you may serve either with carrots or turnips neatly cut and fry'd, instead of capers.

SHEEPS TONGUES EN GRATIN

Des langues de mouton en gratin

These are first stewed tender in a braize, too, peel them, and trim nicely; provide for your sauce three or four fat livers of fowls, or two of a turkey; boil them well, and pound them; put them into a stewpan with a ladle of cullis stirred well, and pass it through an etamine; if you make use of plate pour it into your dish, seasoned with a little pepper and salt and shallot, and set your tongues in, keeping of it stewed over a chaffing-dish of charcoal, cover close down until it is almost dry, pour in a little gravy, with the juice of a lemon or orange, and serve up with a sprinkle of fine minced parsley; if you must do it in a stewpan, lay it smooth in your dish, and put your gravy over it, as directed before.

Lambs tongues are done in the same manner, and make as fashionable a dish.

LAMBS HEADS, WITH SAUCE OF PARSLEY JUICE

Des têtes d'agneaux au jus de persil

Provide two heads of house lambs, take out the under jawbones, and the bone in the neck, cut out the eyes, and chop off the nostrils, wash them well, and let them lay in water an hour, blanch them in water, put them into a little soup pot, pour enough water to cover them, skim it well, and season with an onion, carrot, a bunch of herbs and parsley, whole pepper and mace; to preserve their whiteness you must put in a bit of butter and flour mixt, a sliced lemon, and a morsel of sewet, let 'em boil gently till very tender; and provide your sauce with a ladle of broth well seasoned, dash in a glass of white wine, a bit of butter and flour to thicken it, pepper, salt, and nutmeg; provide some juice of parsley, boil all a few minutes, dish up your heads, taking the skull-bones off with the point of your knife, peel the tongues, and take care not to break the brains, squeeze in the juice of lemon or orange, and serve them up.

Sheep or lambs trotters are frequently done in the same manner, or with a brown sauce, and no bad dish they make.

LAMBS SWEETBREADS, WITH TOPS OF ASPARAGUS

Des ris d'agneaux aux points d'asperges

Blanch your sweetbreads, and put into cold water awhile, put them into a stewpan with a ladle of broth, with pepper, salt, a small bunch of green onions and parsley, and a blade of mace, stir in a bit of butter with flour, and stew all about half an hour; make ready a liaison of two or three eggs and cream, with a little minced parsley and nutmeg; put in your points of asparagus that I suppose to be boiled, and pour in your liaison, and take care it don't curdle; add some juice of lemon or orange and send it to table.

You may make use of pease, young gooseberries, or kidney-beans for this, and all make a pretty dish.

LAMBS EARS, WITH SORREL

Des oreilles d'agneaux a l'oseille

In London such things as these, or calves ears, tails, or the ears of sheep ready for use, or perhaps in some other great markets, are always to be had of the butchers or tripemen.

About a dozen of lambs ears will make a small dish, and they must be stewed tender in a braize; take a large handful of sorrel, chop it a little, and stew it in a spoonful of broth and a morsel of butter, pour in a small ladle of cullis, a little pepper and salt, and nutmeg; stew it a few minutes, and dish up the ears upon it, nicely twisted up.

THE GRISTLES OF A BREAST OF VEAL, WITH A WHITE SAUCE

Des tendrons de veau au blanc

About the half of a breast of veal will do for this small dish; take off all the upper part, and cut the gristles in small bits, blanch them, and put into a stewpan to a ladle of broth; stew it very tender, and put a bit of butter mixt with flour, a bunch of onions and parsley, a blade of mace, pepper and salt; for your sauce you may prepare either pease, asparagus, make a liaison as before, and just before you serve pour it in; add the juice of a lemon, and dish it up.

Breasts of lamb are done in the same manner, and make a favourite dish.

VEAL PALLETS, WITH CHAMPAGNE

Des pallets de veau au vin de Champagne

Provide about two pallets, and boil half an hour, take off the skins, and cut them into such pieces as your pallets of beef, put them into a stewpan with a glass of Champagne, a little minced green onion, parsley, pepper and salt, toss it often till the wine is gone, pour in a ladle of your cullis mixt with gravy, stew 'em softly in it till very tender, dash in a small glass more of your wine, add the juice of a lemon or orange, and send it up.

A FRICASEE OF CALVES TONGUES, WITH CAULIFLOWERS

Une fricasée des langues de veau aux aschon fleurs

Get two tongues, which is enough for a small dish; boil them till the skin comes well off the ragged parts, and slice them very thin, put into a stewpan with a ladle or two of broth, and put in a bunch of onions and parsley, a blade of mace, pepper and salt; let all stew softly till very tender, and liaison as before prescribed, pour it in when boiling hot, cover it close, and let it remain so till your time of dining; move it upon a stove for a minute or two, squeeze in a lemon or orange, and dish it up.

CALVES EARS, WITH LETTUCE

Des oreilles de veau aux laitües

Six ears will do; stew them very tender in a braize, and your lettuce must be done thus, take as many as you have ears and blanch them in water, open the leaves, and put into each a bit of the middling bacon, with a clove or two stuck in each, close the leaves over, and bind with packthread, put them into a stewpan with a ladle of your cullis, and a little gravy, pepper, salt, and a morsel of shallot, stew them till very tender; take your ears out, and clear them from grease, and put them to your leaves, add the juice of a lemon, and serve them up; take care your lettuce are preserved whole, and laid between the ears.

Lambs ears may be done so, too.

VEAL SWEETBREADS WITH MUSHROOMS

Des ris de veau aux champignons

Provide two or three veal sweetbreads, blanch them, and cut them in slices, get a few nice button mushrooms cleaned upon a bit of flannel, put them into a stewpan together, and let them stew gently for half an hour in a ladle of cullis, but put no gravy, for the mushrooms will produce some liquor, take a knot or two, or the yolks of three or four hard eggs, dash in a glass of white wine, a morsel of green onion and parsley minced fine, pepper, salt, and nutmeg, squeeze in the juice of a lemon or orange, and serve it up.

Lambs sweetbreads just so.

CALVES TAILS WITH CARROTS. BROWN SAUCE

Des queues de veau aux carrots. Sauce brune

Cut the tails into two or three pieces, and you must stew these in a braize, and cut the carrots into neat genteel pieces, blanch them a few minutes, take the tails out, and soak the fat well off, put them into a stewpan, with a ladle or two of cullis, carrots, a bunch of basil, onions, thyme and parsley, pepper, salt, a blade of mace, and a clove of rocombole, stew all till your carrots are tender, sprinkle in a little minced parsley, take out the rocombole and herbs, add the juice of lemon or orange, and send it to table.

CALVES BRAINS WITH RICE

Des cervelles de veau au ris

The brains of two heads is enough for a good dish, but an *Hors d'oeuvres* in particular, blanch them, and take off the little bloody fibres, cut into two pieces each, and soak them in a marinade of white wine and vinegar, &c., for an hour, put them into a stewpan with some cullis and gravy, and stew them softly about half an hour; boil your rice in water a few minutes, strain it off, and stew it in broth till it is tender, with a little salt and a bit of mace, dish up the brains, and pour some of the sauce to the rice, squeeze in a lemon or orange, and pour over for serving to table.

When you procure two or three pairs of eyes they make an excellent dish done in the manner of doing the sweetbreads.

TEALS WITH OLIVES

Des cercelles aux olives

Two is enough; when you draw them save the livers, and make a little forcemeat, adding some scrap'd bacon, a mushroom or two, a pretty many herbs, pepper, salt, some shallot, all minced, and well mixt, put into the bellies of your fowls and fasten them up; fry them gently a little while in a hot marinade, and spit them across your spit upon a lark-spit, cover with bacon and paper, and roast them, but not too much; prepare your sauce with a ladle of cullis and gravy mixt, pepper, salt, and shallot, and about a couple of dozen of olives pared; draw off your teals, and put them into your sauce, cut them first down the breast, stew about five minutes; squeeze in plenty of orange, with a few strips of the peel, and send to table.

PARTRIDGES IN RAGOUT, WITH ORANGES

Des perdreaux en ragout, aux oranges

Truss your partridges, and roast in the English way, only use no flour; make a sauce of the livers pounded, and add two or three of chickens, put it into a stewpan with a green onion or two, a mushroom, pepper and salt, and parsley; boil all in cullis a few minutes, and strain through your etamine; cut the partridges as for a fricasee, and put to your sauce; let it boil but just long enough to make the meat hot through, strip in a morsel or two of the peel, a bit of minced shallot and parsley, squeeze in a good deal of juice, and dish it up. Garnish with oranges in quarters.

PARTRIDGES HASH'D, WITH ROCOMBOLE SAUCE

Des perdreaux hachée, sauce au rocombole

Truss these as to roast them in the English way; make a forcemeat with the livers, &c., and roast gently with a lard of bacon and paper, lodge a bit or two of rocombole upon the breasts, and when done, cut all the flesh from the breasts, and cut it in slices thin as posssible; keep your carcasses hot, and provide a sauce for the hash, with a ladle of cullis, minced rocombole, pepper, salt, and nutmeg; boil this a few minutes, and put in your hash; when your dinner is ready put it to the sauce; make it only boiling hot, throw in a little parsley, squeeze in some lemon or orange, and dish up upon the bones or carcasses; put enough of your cullis that some may flow over into the dish.

Woodcocks make a good dish done in this fashion.

SALMY OF WOODCOCKS

Salmis des becasses

For this too the French truss their cocks in the English way, and half roast them, without flour; cut them in fricasee pieces, and take care to secure all the inside except the gizzards and galls, which you must be sure to take clean away, but the ropes, livers, &c., pound to a paste, with a morsel of shallot, green onion and parsley, pepper, salt, and nutmeg, put in a ladle of your cullis, a glass of red wine, and pass it thro' your etamine, pour it into a stewpan to your meat, let it stew very gently for three quarters of an hour, fling in a little minced parsley, the juice of an orange, and serve it up garnish'd with fry'd bread, and some bits in the dish.

Any sort of birds, such as snipes, quails, &c., that are not drawn, make a pleasing dish done in the same manner.

WOODCOCKS WITH FORCEMEAT, WITH CLEAR GRAVY

Des becasses farcez, au jus clair

For this you should draw your cocks, cut off the feet, and truss the thighs in; preserve the ropes for the forcemeat, and make a little mince of your livers, with a morsel of ham, seasoned with a mushroom, pepper, salt and parsley; cut almost all the meat from the breasts of your cocks, cut it in little bits with the ropes, scrape a little bacon and fry it, seasoned with a mushroom or two, a bit of green onion, a little parsley, pepper, salt, and nutmeg, and put to the soft of half a roll soak'd in cream; mix all well with two or three eggs, fill up the breasts in shape as they were, nigh as you can, brush them over with egg and crumbs of bread, and bake them in a slow oven; and for your sauce have ready some clear gravy, with a little shallot, pepper and salt, squeeze in the juice of an orange, and serve them up hot.

BREAST OF FOWLS A LA BINJAMELE

Poitrine des poulardes a la Benjamele

Two fowls make two dishes, but in different ways; cut off the legs whole with the feet, and the next shall give directions how to manage them. But the breasts you must roast, but without the pinions, they may serve for something else; when roasted, take off the skin, and cut off the white flesh, slice it in thickish pieces, put it into a stewpan, and provide your sauce as follows; take about half a pint of cream, a bit of butter mixt with flour, put in a green onion or two whole, a little parsley, pepper and salt, stir it over a slowish fire till it boils to its thickness, and pass it through an etamine, put it to your fowl in a stewpan, and then boil it till it is hot through; add nothing more than the juice of an orange, and send it up.

This sauce may serve for any sort of white meat, and is now very much in fashion.

BALONS OF LEGS OF FOWLS

Des petits balons aux cuisses des poulardes

This is to be done with the four legs; take out the thigh and legbone to the knee, without cutting the skin; let the feet continue on, and scald or burn off the stocking, but take care not to burn or scald the skin, for it is to be sewed up; lay them a little while in a marinade of white wine and vinegar, &c., prepare a forcemeat, such as is for several things before, and spread over the insides; draw them up nice and round, and stew them in a little braize for an hour, or a little more; make a neat sauce of a ladle of cullis and gravy, a dash of white wine, a bit of shallot and parsley minced; take your balons out upon a cloth to drain, and clean from fat; dish them up with the feet to them; boil your sauce a minute, and squeeze in the juice of an orange or lemon, and send it up.

PIGEONS A LA DUXELLE

Des pigeonneaux a la duxelle

Four or five pigeons will do for an *Hors d'oeuvres*; but this is most times served for an *entrée*; cut off the feet and pinions, and slit them down the breast, then take out the livers, and flat them with a cleaver; make a hot marinade of some scraped bacon, seasoned with a mushroom or two, green onions, pepper, salt, thyme and parsley, and a little nutmeg; fry all a few minutes, and let the pigeons be heated through in it, and let them remain till you put them upon your gridiron; take a thin slice of ham for each pigeon, and put them broiling with the ham always at top; I mean when you turn your pigeons, turn your ham upon them;

for your sauce, take a ladle of gravy, some sweet basil, a little thyme, parsley, and shallot, minced very fine, a few slices of mushrooms, boiled all together a few minutes; dish up your breasts downwards, let your ham continue upon them, and pour your sauce over, with the juice of a lemon or orange.

N.B. There's another way of doing this dish, by tying a slice of veal on one side of the pigeon, and ham on the other, and done in a braize; but it is very troublesome and expensive, and I think not better.

FRICASEE OF CHICKENS, WITH WHITE MUSHROOMS

Fricasée des petit poulets, aux champignons blanc

Cut your chickens as before directed, and blanch them in water, only wash off the skim and soil neat and clean, (for the goodness of this dish half depends upon its decent appearance); any body can make it taste well, but it must be a good cook to make it look well; put a bit of butter in your stewpan, just melt it, and put in your chickens, and shake in as much fine flour as will thicken about a pint of broth, keep it toss'd over your stove two or three minutes, and pour in your broth, but keep it moving for a while that it may not be lumpy, put in a bunch of two or three onions and parsley, a little pepper, salt, and a blade of mace, stew it softly about an hour, provide a liaison of three or four eggs, with a spoonful of broth and cream, nutmeg and parsley; put in a few stew'd button mushrooms; make it boiling, and put in the liaison, give it a toss, cover it close till dinner is ready, squeeze in a lemon or orange, and serve it up.

Instead of mushrooms you may put points of asparagus, young pease, and sometimes without either.

SNIPES WITH PURSLAIN LEAVES

Des becassines aux feuilles de pourpier

Draw your snipes, and make a forcemeat for the inside, but your ropes preserve for your sauce, spit 'em across upon a lark-spit, covered with bacon and paper, and roast them gently; for your sauce you must take some prime thick leaves of purslain, blanch them well in water, put them into a ladle of cullis and gravy, a bit of shallot, pepper, salt, nutmeg and parsley, and stew all together for half an hour gently, have the ropes ready blanch'd, and put in; dish up your snipes upon thin slices of bread fry'd, squeeze the juice of an orange into your sauce, and serve it up.

RISOLES OF THE FLESH OF A WOODCOCK, OR SNIPES

Des petits risoles de becasse, ou becassines

Take the flesh from your woodcock, or snipes, and make a forcemeat as follows: Chop your flesh and rope raw and separate, a bit of ham cut very thin, cut into slips, and then into as small morsels as you can, a bit of good sewet, a bit of a manchet soak'd in gravy, season with a bit of green onion, sweet basil and parsley, and a jot of rocambole, pepper, salt and nutmeg, mix all well together, (but not pounded) with an egg or two; lay it in lumps upon a nice thin paste, and make them in the shape of a raspberry or quince puff, but very small; when your dinner is almost ready, provide a large stewpan with lard, and fry all at once; then serve them hot to table without any sauce.

PETTY PATTÉES IN CUPS. WITH A BENJAMELE SAUCE

Des petits pattées en timbal. Sauce a la Benjamele

These are made in copper cups lined with a thin paste; take the breast of a roast chicken, partridge, or a sweetbread blanch'd, and cut into small dice, a slice or two of ham cut in the same manner, two or three girkins, a mushroom or two, or green morelle, fry all this together gently in a little scraped bacon, seasoned with a bit of shallot, green onion, pepper, salt and nutmeg; when cold fill up your cups, and cover with the same paste, bake them gently about half an hour; prepare your sauce, *a la Benjamele*, as for the breast of a fowl. Dish them up bottom uppermost; cut a lid off, and fill them up; take care it is sent very hot to table.

FILLETS OF SOLES, WITH HERBS IN A BROWN SAUCE

Des fillets des soles aux fines herbes brune

Skin your soles both sides, and lay them a while in a marinade of white wine, &c., dry them well in a cloth and fry them without butter or flour, of a nice colour; take off your fillets nicely, cut them into pieces in length about two inches, put them into a stewpan with a glass of Champagne or Rhenish, pepper, salt and nutmeg, a small ladle of gravy and cullis mixt; mince separate, a green truffle or mushroom, a leaf or two of pimpernel, a little sweet basil, thyme and parsley, and a morsel of shallot; put into your gravy, &c. such a quantity of each as you like best; stew all together very gently for a quarter of an hour, squeeze in the juice of a lemon or orange, and serve it up very hot.

The fillets of plaice tenderly handled make a pretty dish in the same way; the flesh is not so firm as soles, which is my reason for this caution. If *maigre* days, instead of cullis or gravy, make a sauce of such small fish as is before prescribed, or a cullis of crawfish.

FILLETS OF WHITINGS MARINADED, AND FRY'D WITH PARSLEY

Fillets des merlans marinez et frite au persil

The fillets of about six smallish whitings is enough; each makes but two from top to bottom; lay them in a marinade of wine, &c. about an hour, dry them well, and toss them in a heap of fine flour, provide a large stewpan of lard, make it hot, and fry all together upon a brisk fire; fry your parsley crisp and green, and serve your fish up upon it. This is a most favourite dish, and generally eat with the juice of an orange or lemon; but some choose what the French call *sauce pouvrade*, or *sauce pour-homme*, which shall be seen by and by provided for the roast and *entremets*.

FRICASEE OF TENCH, WITH WHITINGS LIVERS

Fricasée des tenches, aux fois des merlans

In the whiting season you may have plenty of livers at any fishmonger's shop, and a vast addition it is to the goodness and beauty of any dish of this sort; split your tench, or a brace, according to the size; take out the backbone, and cut the flesh in pieces, so as to make them answer, if you have occasion, to your soles or whitings, toss them up in a bit of melted butter oiled, and a little flour, for a minute or two, pour in a ladle of broth, and a glass of white wine, keep it moving upon the stove till ready to boil, and season with a bunch of green onions and parsley, some mace, pepper and salt, blanch your livers, and stew all together about half an hour; have ready a liaison as before mentioned for fricasees, and just before your dinner-time pour it in, and cover it close; before you send it up give it an easy move over the fire for a moment, add the juice of an orange or lemon, and serve it up.

The heads and melts of your fish are favourite bits; so take care they are among the rest.

N.B. The fillets of weavers, perch, soles, or any such firm sort of fish, make a good fricasee, and done in the same manner.

PERCH IN THE DUTCH FASHION

Des perches a l'Hollandoise

Crimp your perch only one gash from end to end, put them into spring-water half an hour, put them into a stewpan with a large glass of white wine, half as much vinegar, plenty of mace, a little pepper and salt, and a bunch of onions and parsley, and some thyme tied together; let them stew gently in this (turning of them once) about twenty minutes, pour as much hot water in as will fill your dish, with a piece of butter mixt with flour, and boil a few minutes longer, take out your herbs, and serve it up with a heap of parsley-leaves over it boiled nice and green. According to my judgment this is a good and delicate dish, and much the best way of dressing perch.

Gudgeons are done in the same manner.

FILLETS OF MACKEREL, WITH FENNEL AND GOOSEBERRIES

Fillets des maquereaux au fenouille and grosseilles

For this the French always boil their mackerel as we do, only adding a little vinegar and a bunch of herbs, take the sides of fillets from the bone, and cut in two pieces; about four is enough for such a dish as here proposed, put them into a stewpan with the melts and roes whole, dash in a glass of white wine, a ladle of cullis and gravy, some minced fennel, green onion and parsley, pepper, salt and nutmeg; stew all about eight or ten minutes; put in about half a pint of scalded young gooseberries whole, squeeze in a lemon or orange, and serve it up hot.

BROILED WEAVERS WITH BAY LEAVES, WITH SAUCE POUVRADE

Des puavivres grilléz, aux feuilles de lauriers, sauce pouvrade

Notch your fish, and lay them in a marinade of white wine and vinegar, &c. and a few bay leaves, let 'em remain an hour, and dry them in a cloth, broil them of a nice brown colour, with a bay leaf or two upon each, and prepare your sauce with a spoonful or two of gravy, a little white wine and vinegar, some shallot, pepper, salt and parsley, boil it but a minute or two, and send it up in a fish-boat or cup, for most chuse these fish with orange or lemon only.

MACKEREL BROIL'D WITH FINE HERBS

Des maquereaux grilléz aux fines herbes

Draw your mackerel without opening the belly part, and cut them down the back from the neck to the tail, but without flatting of them; take fennel, mint, sweet basil, thyme and parsley, mince all very fine, and make a sort of paste with good butter, pepper, salt, and pounded spices, rub it on the flesh of your fish, and place them first upon the gridiron, on the belly part; when the butter is well soak'd in, turn them to the sides, and make them of a good colour; make your sauce of a ladle of cullis and gravy, and a morsel of shallot or rocombole boiled a minute or two, with the juice of an orange or two; support your fish in the dish back uppermost, with some quarters of the same, and pour your sauce in boiling hot. This dish may be served for either an *entrée* or *hors d'oeuvre*, or a remove for a soup.

COLLOPS OF RABBITS, WITH CHAMPAGNE WINE

Des escalopes de lapreaux au vin de Champagne

Take the flesh of a couple of rabbits, cut it in slices, and with a knife pat it down so as to make it very thin, rub some butter all over a large stewpan, mixt with a green onion and some parsley minced very fine, stick the meat round, and fry it a minute or two over a brisk stove, giving it a toss or two, let it lie in that till you have prepared your sauce, which must be thus done, put into a small stewpan, a ladle of cullis, a glass of Champagne, pepper, salt and nutmeg, a small quantity of such herbs as you like, and a morsel of shallot, boil it five or six minutes, and put your rabbit in, make it only boiling hot, squeeze in the juice of a lemon or orange, and serve it up.

The flesh of chickens make a neat dish in the same way.

The
Sea Lobster

ENTREMETS
OR SECOND COURSE DISHES

ENTREMETS

Next are the *Entremets*, or second course dishes, of which I shall put down about forty of the most fashionable; and give a hint of the management of the roast. By roast I mean what is served for second course, such as a leveret, woodcocks, snipes, or partridges, &c. but no large things, and the sauces they usually serve with 'em. As to pastry things I shall put but few, for I think the English in most of them excel.

LAMBS-STONES MARINADED AND FRY'D, WITH PARSLEY

Des alumelles d'agneaux marinéz and frits, au persil

In this dish too, if the French are not too cunning for us, they are more modest, and give it a prettier name; blanch them, and take off the outer skins, lay them in a marinade of white wine and vinegar, &c. an hour, dry them in a cloth, tumble them about well in flour, and fry them of a nice colour, and serve them up with no other sauce but parsley nicely fry'd, under and over them; and if well done it makes a pretty dish for second courses.

PIGEONS AU SOLEIL

Des pigeonneaux au soleil

For this generally is provided squab tame pigeons; blanch them, and stew about an hour in a braize, make them very dry and clean from fat and soil, and make a batter of nothing more than ale or small beer with flour and a morsel of butter oil'd and put into it well stirred together, have a large stewpan of lard ready, dip in your pigeons without cutting off either heads, legs or wings, and fry them of a fine colour, and serve them to table *comme les alumelles*, with parsley. *Sauce pouvrade, sauce pauvre homme*, or *sauce Robert*, should be always ready in a boat or cup, if any of the company should ask; and I'll put 'em down before I finish.

VEAL SWEETBREADS MARINADED AND FRY'D

Des ris de veau frits, and marinéz

Blanch your sweetbreads well, cut them in slices, and lay them in a marinade as before provided, dry 'em well, and prepare three or four eggs, the yolks and whites beat well together, have plenty of crumbs of bread, dip your sweetbreads in, and bread them well; do them a second time in the same manner, make them nice and smooth, and fry them as your pigeons, and serve them up with a heap of parsley under and round; for it adds greatly to the pretty aspect of the dish, and costs nothing.

ROASTED SWEETBREADS, WITH ASPARAGUS

Des ris de veau rotis, aux asperges

Two good sweetbreads are enough for this small dish; blanch them, and lay them in a marinade as before, spit them tight upon a lark-spit, and tie them to another, a slice of bacon upon each, and covered with paper; when almost done take that off, and pour a drop of butter upon them, with a few crumbs of bread, and roast them of a nice colour; take two bunches of asparagus, and boil, not so much as we boil them to eat with butter; dish up your sweetbreads and your grass between them, take a little cullis and gravy, with a jot of shallot and minced parsley, boil it a few minutes, squeeze in the juice of a lemon or orange, and serve it up.

LAMBS-STONES EN GRATIN

Des alumelles en gratin

Blanch your alumelles well, and take off the outer skins, and cut 'em in thin slices; make your sauce of the fat livers of turkeys or fowls, pound them well; after blanching, put them to the cullis and gravy as before, season with a morsel of green onion, mushroom, thyme, basil and parsley, pepper, salt, and nutmeg; pass it through your etamine, pour it into a stewpan to your meat, stew all a few minutes, add the juice of a lemon or orange, and serve it up.

SHEEPS RUMPS FRY'D

Des queues de mouton frites

This is begun in the manner of your rumps before; i.e. in a braize, drain and dry them well in a cloth; prepare for this as for your sweetbreads fry'd, and serve them up in the same manner; but take care they are done very tender, or you may as well eat a bit of the sheep's skin.

Lambs rumps are as well this way.

RAGOUT MELÉ, WITH ASPARAGUS OR PEASE

Ragout melé, aux asperges, ou pois

For this dish you may preserve enough of matters you have to make your dish; you should provide two or three livers, a knot or two of eggs, some morsels of ham, cocks-stones and combs, well stewed; add to this a few mushrooms or morelles, and season with a little shallot, parsley, and pepper and salt; pour to all this in a stewpan a ladle of gravy and cullis; let all stew together for about half an hour; put in the juice of a lemon or orange, and serve it up hot with or without orange as you like best.

FAT LIVERS WITH FORCEMEAT

Des fois gras farcéz

Four or five large livers of turkeys will do for this dish; blanch them in water two or three minutes, and make a forcemeat of some livers of chickens, a bit of ham, a mushroom, a morsel of

onion and parsley, pepper, salt and a few crumbs of bread, grate
in a little nutmeg, mince all fine, work it up to a paste with a
couple of eggs, and fill up the open part of your livers, and make
them nice and plump, brush over with an egg, and some crumbs
of bread, and bake them half an hour in a gentle oven; for your
sauce take a ladle of cullis and gravy, three or four thin slices of
ham, a little pepper and salt, a morsel of shallot, boil all about
five minutes, squeeze in a lemon or orange, and send them to
table with the ham upon or between them.

CHICKENS FEET WITH FORCEMEAT

Des pats de poulet farcéz

When you make a fricasee, or any such thing, preserve the feet
to make a dish of this sort; strip off the stockings by scalding,
tie them up in a bundle, and stew them in a braize, boil them
very tender with a little seasoning, dry them in a cloth, and
prepare such a forcemeat as for your balons, above; fill up the
claws with it, dip them into some beaten eggs, and crumb them
well; do it a second time, and press it well on, and fry them in
plenty of lard, and serve them up without any sauce in the dish,
with a heap of fry'd parsley under them.

Fowls or chickens feet make a pretty second dish done many different ways, either in a little brown sauce, with asparagus tops,
pease, artichoke bottoms, &c. or in a fricasee, or white sauce of
any kind.

PINIONS, WITH A SHARP SAUCE

Des elerons, au sauce piquant

The French always cut off the pinions of all the fowls they dress, roasted or not, so that a reserve of these things may be always made for such a small dish as this, and few people value them roasted; blanch them, and do them in the same way as your feet; either in a braize, or otherwise stewed tender; for your sauce take a little of every strong herb you get, minced very fine, a morsel of onion and shallot to a ladle of gravy and cullis, pepper and salt; boil all together for a quarter of an hour, squeeze plenty of orange or lemon, with a dash of Champagne or other white wine, and send it up.

PITHS, OR MARROW OF THE BACK, OR CHINE OF A CALF, FRY'D

Des amourettes de veau frites

Cut your piths in lengths about three or four inches, blanch them in water, and take off the outermost skin, lay them an hour in a marinade of white wine and vinegar, &c. dry them in a cloth, make a batter of ale or small beer, pour in a little oil or oiled butter, stir it well together, put in your piths, and give them a toss, and fry them of a beautiful yellow, and dish them up on a heap of fry'd parsley.

Piths of mutton or lamb makes as pretty a dish.

HOGS EARS A LA ST. MENHOULT, THE FEET FRY'D

Des oreilles de cochon a la St. Menhoult, les pieds frits

One pair of feet and ears for this is quite enough; blanch them in water, split the feet, and with a couple of slices of bacon, and a flat stick like a bit of a lath, tie them together again to keep of a neat shape, stew them in a braize separate from any thing else, till they are very tender, strip the ears as fine as possible; and for your sauce take a large onion cut very thin in slices, and fry brown in a bit of butter, strain them off, and put them into a clean stewpan to the ears with a ladle of cullis, a dash of white wine, pepper and salt; let it stew a quarter of an hour, with a morsel of shallot, a spoonful of good mustard, squeeze in a lemon or orange, add a little minced parsley, and dish up with your feet fry'd in the same manner as your sheeps rumps, to lay round.

EGGS A LA PROVINÇALE, WITH CULLIS

Eggs a la provinçale, au coulis

Take eight or nine eggs (leave out two or three of the whites) and beat them well, put in half a ladle of cullis, a morsel of green onion and parsley minced, pepper, salt and nutmeg, stir it over a slow fire till it is thick enough in the dish, squeeze in the juice of a lemon or orange; dish it up; garnish with some bits of bread fry'd of a nice colour.

EGGS AU MIROIR

Des oeuffs au miroir

For this you must have a dish that will bear the fire, rub the bottom with a bit of butter or oil, sprinkle a morsel of green onion and parsley minced, a little pepper, salt and nutmeg, set your dish upon a chaffing-dish of charcoal, break in as many fresh eggs as will almost fill it, pour over them as much cream as your dish will well hold; when it is just boiling dash with a spoon the cream over the tops, that they may be equally done, squeeze in the juice of an orange or lemon, and serve it up.

EGGS AU SOLEIL

Des oeuffs au soleil

Poach about eight fresh eggs very nicely, take them out into cold water (not draw cold water to the hot, for in a moment they'll all stick to the bottom), lay them a while in a marinade of a glass of wine and vinegar, &c. dry them upon a cloth, prepare a batter of ale, &c. as before prescribed, fry them nicely in lard, and serve them up upon a deal of fry'd parsley.

EGGS SAUCE A LA BENJAMELE

Des oeuffs sauce a la Benjamele

Poach about as many for this dish and order in the same manner; but be sure they are fresh; for, from the experience I have had, I am sure it is not in the power of the best cook in the kingdom to poach stale ones handsome, notwithstanding they may come all whole out of the shell; get your sauce as before mentioned, put the eggs in when it is only warm, and just before you serve it to table squeèze in the juice of an orange or lemon, give it a moment's heat; dish up, pouring over the sauce, and a small pinch of pepper upon each egg.

EGGS A LA TRIPE FRICASEED

Des oeuffs a la tripe en fricasée

Take about seven or eight eggs, and boil hard, but not too hard, for there is nothing has a more offensive smell than eggs boiled too long, ten minutes is enough; put them into cold water, and peel them nicely, cut each into about six slices, melt a bit of butter in a stewpan, put in a little minced onion and parsley, pepper, salt and nutmeg; put your eggs gently in, that the yolk may not separate from the white, put in half a ladle of broth, with a morsel of butter and flour, boil it very softly, prepare a liaison of eggs, &c. and a minute or two before your dinner time pour it in, gently moving it over a slow fire, squeeze in some juice, and send it up.

This is a favourite dish among the French and other foreigners, and some times done with a cullis instead of this white sauce, with a little oil and sweet herbs.

EGGS POACHED, WITH A SAUCE OF MINCED HAM

Des oeuffs pochéz au jambon mincéz

Poach some eggs as before; for your sauce take two or three slices of boiled ham, or a slice or two raw, and well blanched, mince it very fine, a mushroom, a girkin, a morsel of onion, a little parsley, pepper and nutmeg; stew all together a quarter of an hour; when it is your time of serving to table, let your sauce be about half boiling, and put in your eggs, squeeze in the juice of an orange or lemon, dish up, and pour your sauce over.

This is a good dish with tops of asparagus, or pease done in manner like this, leaving out the minced things. There are numberless ways of dressing eggs, so that it would be endless to put all down here. Eggs with gravy, spinach, sorrel, asparagus, broccoli, are pretty second course dishes, and many others that I could name; but they are grown so very common I shall not give them place here.

SMELTS WITH ANCHOVIES AND CAPERS

Des eperlans aux anchois and capres

About eight large smelts is enough for a little dish; for your sauce boil a couple of anchovies in a glass of Rhenish or other white wine till it is dissolved, and strain to a ladle of cullis and gravy, season with a bunch of onions and parsley, a blade of mace, and a bay leaf or two, pepper and salt, put your fish in, and let 'em stew gently about a quarter of an hour, take out your onions and parsley, and throw in a spoonful of capers, make all boiling hot, squeeze in some juice of orange or lemon; take your fish out to dish up, very tenderly, fling in a little minced parsley to your sauce, and pour it over; garnish with orange or lemon in quarters.

You cannot name a small freshwater fish that is not good done this way.

GUDGEONS EN GRATIN, WITH LIVERS OF WHITINGS

Des goujons en gratin, aux fois de merlans

About a quarter of a hundred of gudgeons will do; provide for your sauce a few livers of whitings; if not to be had easily take the liver of a skaite or thornback, thoroughly blanch it well, take a ladle of cullis and gravy, an onion or two, some parsley, a bit of mace, pepper and salt, and a mushroom, put in your liver or livers, boil all a quarter of an hour or so, and pass it through an etamine, put it to your fish, and stew them gently fifteen or twenty minutes, squeeze in the juice of a lemon or orange, dish up your gudgeons in neat order, and pour your sauce over.

This is best where plate is used, and done over a chaffing-dish, that the sauce may stick to the bottom, and moistened afterwards with a little gravy; it takes its name from that, and an excellent sauce it is for such little matters; and, was I a gentleman, I would keep two or three silver dishes in my house, if it was for no other use but this; and some little creams require it too, which you will have among these entremets.

CRAWFISH, WITH THE SPAWN OR EGGS OR A LOBSTER

Des ecrevisses aux oeuffs de mer

A quarter of a hundred of crawfish is enough for this dish; take the shells off from the tails and the small claws, pound them well with some of the spawn (the inside spawn is best to add to the colour) pour to it a spoonful or two of broth or gravy, with some cullis, and rub it well through an etamine, put it to your fish, with a blade of mace, pepper and salt, a little nutmeg; stew all together a few minutes, squeeze in the juice of a lemon or orange, and serve it up.

PRAWNS WITH BUTTER, OR BUTTERED PRAWNS

Des crevettes au beurre

Take the tails only of the prawns, and peel them, pick out the little sand beg or maw from the body, and pound them all with a little pepper and a morsel of onion and nutmeg; put into them a spoonful or two of broth, and pass through an etamine; to two ounces of good butter add as much fine flour as will thicken it, toss it over a stove two or three minutes, squeeze in the juice of a lemon or orange, and send it up hot.

Small lobsters make a very pretty and good dish done in the same manner, but be sure you take out the maw of the body and gravelly gut of the tail, or you must spoil your dish.

On fish days make a little broth of fish.

FORCEMEAT OF LOBSTERS IN THE SHELLS

Des ecrevisses de mer farcéz dans les coquilles

Two middle-sized lobsters will do for this dish; take the tails with the soft part of the insides, and chop very small, put to it the flesh of a plaice, and pound all together, but only to mix it well, grate in a little nutmeg, pepper, a spoonful of oil and vinegar, minced parsley, the soft of a bit of bread soak'd in broth or cream, a couple of eggs, stir all well together, cut the body shells in two pieces longways, trim them neatly, and fill them with your forcemeat, brush them over with a little butter and egg, strew a few crumbs of bread over, and bake them in a slow oven about half an hour; squeeze on the juice of orange or lemon, and serve them up hot. Taste this before you put it into the shell, for it may not be salt enough. The reason of omitting this ingredient with shellfish is, they are always boiled in salt and water.

PEASE WITH CREAM

Des petits pois a la creme

Let your pease be very young, put them into a stewpan with a bit of bacon with some cloves stuck in, pour in a ladle of broth, a bunch of onions and parsley, pepper, and a little salt if it is required, stew them gently till almost dry, take out the bacon and herbs, and put about a gill of cream, a bit of butter and flour mixt, let it go gently on about ten minutes, squeeze in the juice of lemon or orange, and dish them up very hot. Sometimes I have seen Mr. Clouet put in a bit of fine sugar, and in the English way of stewing pease I have never seen it done without.

Des pois aux laittües brune

Pease with brown lettuce differs only by chopping some cabbage-lettuce and mixing with them, and instead of cream use a ladle of cullis. But the Old English way of dressing pease with a bit of good butter I think is still the best.

ASPARAGUS WITH CLEAR GRAVY

Des asperges au jus clair

For this, trim and scrape your grass neat and clean, set them over the fire in but little cold water and salt: the reason of this is, the French prefer a crispness and yellow in asparagus and French beans, to what we are always in so much care to make green and tender; but they eat it (as they do many other vegetables) for a hot sallet; boil your grass but a little time, and serve them to table with nothing but gravy and the juice of oranges or lemons.

French beans whole are done in the same manner frequently.

FRENCH BEANS, WITH A WHITE SAUCE

Des haricots au blanc

For this the French cut their beans as thin as possible, and boil as we do in a vast deal of water, with salt, to preserve their greenness, but not so tender, strain them off, and put 'em to a small ladle of broth, put in a small bunch of green onions and parsley, with a little pepper and salt, just bring it to boiling; prepare a liaison of eggs, &c. and pour in, toss it over the fire a minute, add the juice of a lemon or orange, and serve it up.

FRICASEE OF MUSHROOMS

Des champignons en fricasée

Clean some nice button mushrooms with a flannel and water, wash them in a second, and put them into a stewpan, with a glass of Champagne, Rhenish, or other white wine, a bunch of onions, thyme and parsley, pepper, salt, and a blade of mace, toss them up in this upon a stove a few minutes, and pour a small ladle of broth, with a bit of butter mixt with flour; let all stew a quarter of an hour, take out your herbs, have ready a liaison as before, and just before your dinner-time pour it in, move it gently over the stove a minute, squeeze in an orange or lemon, and dish it up.

Green morelles are done in the same manner, and give an excellent flavour in all made dishes and forcemeats, but they are not to be had but a month or two in the year. Your dry'd morelles and truffles from abroad are like what we call a chip in potrage; they do neither harm nor good.

TRUFFLES IN FRENCH WINE

Des truffles au vin de France

Truffles in England are a very scarce commodity, and of consequence very dear; but are sometimes to be had. I have known some found in the neighbourhood where I live, but very bad, and not much preferable to a potatoe. The good and best are from some part of Italy, where they make dishes of them many different ways; but the only method of dressing them here is, first of all to lay them to soak some time in water, and brush them with a hard brush, for they grow in a stiff clayey ground, so that it is no easy matter to make them clean. Put them into as much claret or Burgundy as will cover them, a large onion or two, a bunch of herbs, whole pepper, salt, and some spices; let 'em simmer gently for about half an hour, and send them to table hot in a napkin; pepper and salt is the general sauce for them; preserve your wine they are boil'd in, it gives an excellent flavour to cullis or gravy, &c.

CARDOONS, WITH PIQUANT SAUCE

Des cardons, sauce piquante

Cardoons are a thistley sort of vegetables, and an exotick plant, and are managed in the garden as celery or endives, by being moulderd up as they grow in height to make them white. The French make use of this in some sort of sauces in the first-course dishes instead of celery, &c. But for an *entremets*, or second-course dish, they generally do it in the following manner: One large one is enough for a small dish; cut the white part only in pieces about two inches long, blanch it in water, and if you have a braize tie it up, and stew it very tender in that; if not take broth, season it high, and stew it in that; take it out upon a cloth, and pull of the skin on both sides, and put it into a sauce piquant, as before mentioned; let stew softly twenty minutes or half an hour, squeeze in the juice of a lemon or orange, and dish it up. This is very good sauce for roast beef or mutton.

SHERDOONS, A LA BENJAMELE

Des sherdons, a la Benjamele

This is a plant of our own, and grows common upon dry banks and barren ground, but worth nothing for this use till improved by the gardener, which is done by transplanting, and earthing up to whiten, and when peeled, and brought to market, looks more like fine endive than a common thistle. The English always plain boil it, and have butter only for sauce; but foreigners with the sauce above, or a brown sauce of cullis or gravy; boil it in a little broth, pepper and salt, but not tender; pour that from it, and put your white sauce, let stew a few minutes, squeeze in an orange or lemon, and dish it up. Whole heads of celery and endives are often done in the same way for these *entremets*; and most foreigners eat heartily of them.

FRY'D ARTICHOKES MARINADED

Des artichaux marinéz

Trim them to the sound part of the bottom, and cut off the small leaves round, cut the points of the others to about an inch above the bottom, cut them in small pieces, and take out the choke or seedy part, lay them to soak in a marinade of white wine and vinegar, &c. often moving them; prepare a batter of beer and butter, dry them well, and fry all at once, and send them up upon a heap of fry'd parsley. Fry sometimes with flour sticking to the marinade, and sometimes without any.

BOTTOMS OF ARTICHOKES, WITH A BROWN SAUCE

Des queues d'artichaux, sauce brune

Cut off all the black and soil from the bottom, trim round the sides, but not through the heart of the leaves, cut off the tops of the leaves almost to the bottom, so as to leave a hollow; when your choke is taken out, boil them in water till you find the inside, put them into cold water, and with your finger scrape it out to make 'em white and tender; prepare a hot marinade of boiling water, a lump of butter and flour mixt, a bit of sewet, a lemon peeled and sliced in a little salt, an onion and a bunch of herbs; a little soup-pot is best for this; when it is well mixt and boils, put in your bottoms, and let them simmer sideways till very tender, and they will grow white as a curd; for your sauce take a ladle of cullis, and add to it such sorts of herbs as you like, pepper, salt and nutmeg; boil all a little while, take out the bottoms upon a cloth to drain, dish them up, squeeze the juice of an orange or lemon into your sauce, and send to table.

Here seems to be a vast deal said upon such a trifling matter; but I have been in hundreds of kitchens where there never was a cook that could cut an artichoke-bottom genteelly, or make it white; and there cannot be a prettier dish; and you may serve them to table with a white sauce of any sort, or with plain butter only.

LETTUCE WITH FORCEMEAT

Des laittües farcéz

Blanch your lettuce, and open all the leaves to the heart; take a forcemeat such as is before provided for such little things; put as much into each as you can close; put them into a stewpan with as much broth as will cover them, put pepper, salt, some pounded mace, a bit of butter and flour; provide a liaison of egg and cream, &c., use them easy, squeeze in the juice of a lemon or orange, and dish up hot. Another time make a brown sauce.

SPINAGE WITH CREAM AND EGGS, OR FRY'D BREAD

Des epinars a la creme, aux oeuffs, ou du pain frit

This being a pretty genteel dish, it is pity to leave it out. Scald it in a morsel of butter and water and salt, press the juice from it very dry, chop it small, and put it into a stewpan with about half a pint of cream, a morsel of butter and flour, a whole old onion, pepper and salt, a little nutmeg; stew all together a few minutes, take out your onion, squeeze in a lemon or orange, and dish it up. Garnish with either hard eggs cut in two, or bits of bread nicely fry'd.

A DUTCH CREAM

Une creme a l'Hollandoise

Provide as much cream as will fill your dish, boil it with sugar, a bit of lemon-peel, and some coriander-seed, let it stand to cool, with a quart of cream, take the yolks of ten eggs, make them smooth and put to your cream, rub it through an etamine, have a stewpan of water boiling, put your dish upon it to touch the water, pour in the cream, cover with another dish, and watch when it is settled, set in some cool place, and send it to table, you may colour it with a hot iron if you like. This and the next are often served upon the middle of the table, which is supposed to be a large dish, then take the whites of the eggs, whisk them up to a nice froth, and gently lay on your cream, sift a little fine sugar upon it, colour and take the rawness of the eggs off with a salamander.

CREAM MADE WITH GIZZARDS

Une creme veloutée aux gesiers

Provide as much cream for this dish as is necessary. Without the help of eggs, boil it with such ingredients as the other, but add a pinch of salt, get the gizzards of three or four chickens, take only the skins within side, wash and dry them, that you may roll them to powder, put them into your etamine, and pour in the cream, pass it through three or four times; prepare your dish upon boiling water as before; the moment you see it coming to a curd take it off, and set it in a cool place. This is a pretty *entremets*, and when you would make use of it for a large dish whisp up a little cream into a froth, and serve it up.

Creams of tea, coffee, chocolate, &c., are done in the same manner, only take care you boil them well in a little of your cream, that they have the full flavour.

APPLE FRITTERS A LA BAVARRE

Des bignets de pommes a la Bavarre

Pare and quarter some large pippins, lay them to soak in brandy, fine sugar, cinnamon and lemon-peel, and toss them often. Your dinner being almost ready, dry them in a cloth, tumble about well in fine flour, and fry them all very tender in hogs lard; dish them up, and sift plenty of fine sugar over them, colour nicely with a salamander, and send them up.

PEACH FRITTERS, WITH RHENISH WINE

Des bignets de peches, au vin de Rhin

This must be done with peaches of the fleshy sort, and cut in two, put them to some Rhenish wine as long as you please, with plenty of fine sugar, cinnamon, and lemon-peel, dry 'em, and fry without any flour, strain your wine into another stewpan, and boil it to a caromel; dish up, and pour it over with the kernels of the peaches blanched, split, and thrown in.

Apricots, or any sort of large good fruit, are done in the way as before, with this difference only; you must be very cautious to use them tenderly, and fry them in a thin batter of small beer and flour: there is a fleshy nectarin that makes a fritter, but they too must be fry'd in this batter, for the skin won't bear the violent heat of the lard.

FRITTERS OF CURRANT JELLY

Des bignets de gelée de grosseilles

Of these there are several sorts; but the favourites of Mr. Clouet were one of the pastry sort, and the other I'll shew in my next, Provide a nice rich paste, and roll out very thin; brush it all over with egg, and lay your jelly down in little lumps as many as you may want for a little dish; prepare another sheet of paste, and lay it over, pressing well between, that it may not come out in frying; make your lard pretty hot, and fry of a fine yellowish colour, and dish them up with some fine sugar sifted over.

CURRANT FRITTERS EN SURPRIZE

Des bignets de groseilles en surprize

The difference between this and the last is this: instead of paste, cut some bits of water-paper, and lay some little lumps of jelly upon each, wet round the dges with a little water; but close them up as you go; have ready a thin batter of small beer or ale, and some oiled butter; have your fat ready heated, and put them to fry immediately; take this care and you will make a pretty dish, and serve them up with sugar sifted over.

CHERRIES IN A FRENCH PASTE

Des bignets de cerises au four

For this you must have a conserve of cherries, and your paste make as follows; take half a pint of water, put to it a morsel of fine sugar, a grain of salt and a bit of lemon-peel, an ounce of butter, and boil it a minute or two, take it from your fire, and work in as much fine flour as it takes to a tender paste, put one egg at a time and mould it well till it comes to such a consistence as to pour with the help of a spoon out of the stewpan upon a tin or cover, covered with flour; scrape it off in lumps upon tin with the handle of a large key, and bake them of a nice colour and crispness, cut a hole in the bottom, and fill up with your conserve, sift some sugar over, and dish up.

If you make this paste according to the rule before you, it will swell very large and hollow, and make a genteel *entremets*; and for the next, which is called:

PUFFED FRITTERS

Beignets soufflez

Make the same sort of paste, but rather softer; take a very thin thing to put it upon; have a large stewpan of lard made hot, but not very hot; take the hook of one of your ladles or spoons, dip into the fat, and scrape it into it in little bits; keep them moving well, and you will find 'em swell like those in the oven, cut a little hole in each but not off, croud in a little jelly or conserve, and dish them up with sugar.

These fritters are often sent to table without any thing within-side. Any sort of preserved fruits, raspberries or quinces, &c.

PEARS PORTUGUESE FASHION, WITH CURRANTS

Des poires a la Portugueuse, aux groseilles seches

Take three or four *boncretiens*, or other good winter pears, pare them, cut them in two, and take out the choke, boil them in water only half an hour, put them into a stewpan, pour in a pint of Port wine, with a lump of fine sugar, a stick of cinnamon, a bit of lemon-peel, a spoonful or two of water, and about five or six ounces of the best dry currants; let all stew together till your pears are very tender; dish them up, and pour your currants over, but take out the cinnamon and peel.

The French make several sorts of amlets of eggs; but in these matters I think we beat them all to pieces, except one, and that is this.

AMLET A LA NOAILLES

Une omelette a la Noailles

For a small dish take the yolks of about eight fresh eggs, but save the whites; make the yolks nice and smooth, with a quarter of a pint of thick cream, strew in some sifted fine sugar, crumble in a few drop-cakes or fine biscuit, and a little nutmeg; a few minutes before your dinner-time, whisk up your whites, and stir all together well, moisten your frying-pan first with lard, and made very hot, and pour it in, have a bit of butter by you, and stoop round upon your trevet to do the sides first, move the edges with the point of your knife, and put in some morsels of butter; when it is pretty well set, lay the edges as far as you can to the middle, make it round, and turn it bottom uppermost in your dish, sift on some sugar, and serve it up hot; garnish with orange. Your chief care must be to prevent its sticking to the bottom, fry it nicely, and you will find it a very handsome and good *entremets*.

This may be made with a savoury sauce by putting cullis of meat or fish, with their proper seasonings, instead of cream, &c.

STRAWBERRY FRITTERS

Des beignets aux fraises

For this you must make a batter of another sort from what you have seen before; to two eggs well beat, whites and yolks both, put about half a pint of cream, made thick with fine flour, a little

fine sugar and nutmeg, put your strawberries in raw, and fry them
in a pan of clean lard, a spoonful at a time, dish them up in a
pyramid, and sift sugar between and at top.

This is a pretty way of making fritters with any sort of fruit.

RICE FRITTERS

Des beignets du ris

Take a quarter of a pound of ground rice, and boil tender with
a blade or two of mace in water only till it is quite dry, pour in
a spoonful or two of cream, but it must be very thick; take out
the mace, grease a stewpan with a morsel of fresh butter, put in
the rice, and stir in two ounces of fine powder sugar, put in the
whites only of two or three eggs, and work it well over the fire
till it comes to a paste, spread it upon the bottom of a dish or
cover, well covered with flour, and when cool dash some flour
on, and cut it into small diamonds, roll them up into little balls
the bigness of a marble, and throw them into a heap of flour; provide some lard very hot, take them from the flour, and fry them
very brown, give them a little shake in some powdered sugar,
and send them up.

MACAROONS WITH CREAM

Des macarons a la creme

These are to be had at any confectioner's shop in London, and
the newer they are the better; boil them in water only till very
tender, to half a pint of cream put half a small spoonful of flour,

some sugar and nutmeg, with a morsel of salt, stir it over the fire till it is thickish, cool it, and put in the yolks of three eggs, and a morsel of oiled new butter, stir it well together, and put in your macaroons, put a nice little rim of paste round your dish, pour in your ingredients, and put it to bake about a quarter of an hour, and take care it is of a fine colour; sift a little sugar over it, and serve to table.

This is not what we call macaroons of the sweet biscuit sort, but a foreign paste, the same as vermicelly, but made very large in comparison to that.

MACAROONS WITH PARMESAN CHEESE

Des Macarons au Parmesan

For this too you must boil them in water first, with a little salt, pour to them a ladle of cullis, a morsel of green onion and parsley minced fine, pepper, salt and nutmeg; stew all a few minutes, and pour into a dish with a rim as before, squeeze a lemon or orange, and cover it over pretty thick with Parmesan cheese grated very fine, bake it of a fine colour about as long a time as the last, and serve it up hot.

The French serve to their tables a great many dishes with this sort of cheese, and in the same manner, only sometimes with a savoury white sauce, such as scallops, oysters, and many of the things you have among these *entremets*.

SCALLOPS IN SHELLS, WITH ONIONS

Des escallopes en coquilles, aux onions

Take your scallops from your shells, blanch them well, and take off the beards, provide some small old onions, peel off the two outmost skins, and fry them of a nice colour, and tender, cut the scallops in thin pieces, put them into a stewpan, with the onions well drained, a little cullis, and pepper, salt, parsley and nutmeg; stew all together a few minutes, squeeze the juice of orange or lemon, and put into the shells, sift over a little fine grated bread, but not to hide what it is, colour with a salamander, or in an oven, and serve 'em to table.

This is a genteel good *entremets*, with *sauce a la Benjamele*, with a little Parmesan cheese nicely coloured.

ATTELETS OF OYSTERS, WITH CLEAR GRAVY, BROILED

Des attelettes d'huitres au jus clair, grillée

Blanch your oysters, and take off the beards, prepare some thin slices of bacon, and a sweetbread blanched, and cut in bits the bigness of the oysters, and put them upon skewers, (silver skewers are prettiest) and lay them awhile in a hot marinade of bacon, seasoned with a mushroom, &c., fry'd as before prescribed; when cool rub well in it, and strew plenty of grated bread, boil them of a fine brown, and serve them up with a clear gravy and lemon or orange juice, but don't take the oysters, &c., off the skewers.

You may make such a little dish of what you please; but let all be raw when you put it upon the skewers: you may sometimes fry them in a batter.

ANCHOVIES, WITH PARMESAN CHEESE

Des anchois au Parmesan

Fry some bits of bread about the length of an anchovy in good oil or butter, lay the half of an anchovy, with the bone upon each bit, and strew over them some Parmesan cheese grated fine, and colour them nicely in an oven, or with a salamander, squeeze the juice of an orange or lemon, and pile them up in your dish and send them to table.

This seems to be but a trifling thing, but I never saw it come whole from the table.

OLIVES WITH ROCOMBOLE

Des olives a la rocombole

Take the fleshy part from the kernels, as many as will do for your dish, blanch them a minute or two, put them into a stewpan with a ladle of cullis and gravy, mince in some rocombole and parsley, pepper, salt and nutmeg; let them stew but three or four minutes; dash in a glass of white wine, a spoonful of good oil, squeeze in plenty of lemon or orange, and serve them up.

This too is an *entremets* that is much eat among foreigners, and the English seldom miss of coming in for a share of it.

CUPS OF EGGS, WITH GRAVY OF PARTRIDGE

Des tinbals au jus de perdreaux, aux oeuffs

Take one partridge, and split it down the back, and then notch the breast and legs, put it into a small stewpan with a bit of ham, put in one onion, a carrot, and a little parsley, pour in a spoonful or two of broth, and let stew gently till it is dry and of a fine colour at the bottom, pour in a ladle of broth more, and let boil ten minutes or a quarter of an hour softly, strain it through a lawn sieve, take off the fat, put in a little salt and nutmeg, and pour cool into six or seven eggs well beat, pass it through an etamine, and pour it into five or six China cups, have a stewpan of hot water and set them in; let it boil till you perceive they are set like a custard, and serve up hot.

This is not a bad *entremets* with the gravy extracted from any sort of fowl.

CUPS A L'AMANDE, WITH SWEET BISCUIT

Des tinbals a l'almande, biscuit douce

This is done pretty much in the nature of our custard, but with an addition of several things, and putting no whites of the eggs; take almost a pint of cream, and boil it with some sugar, lemon-peel and coriander-seed, beat the yolks of about seven eggs, and when it is cool put it to it, pass it through your etamine, taste it, and put it into your cups, with a thin slice of biscuit upon each, and set them as the last were done; sift some fine sugar over them, and colour with a hot iron, but take care you don't curdle them.

There are some few cold *entremets* that the French outdo us in, which I shall make bold to add.

PIECE OF BEEF WITH JELLY

Piece de boeuf a la glass

Take a prime piece of the buttock or rump of beef, let it hang some time that it may be the more tender, rub it well with saltpetre and some salt, let it lay four or five days, and water it a little that it may not make your jelly too salt, put it into a pot as nigh as you can, and cover it with water, season with some carrots, onions, herbs, whole pepper and spice, take care to skim it well, and let it simmer very gently till it is very tender; when it is cool take it out, strain your liquor through a lawn sieve, take the fat clean off, and boil it to as much as will cover your meat, beat up to a froth the whites of two or three eggs mixt with it, and pass it through a bag or napkin; the next day it will be a clear jelly; and when you serve the beef to table spread it over it; you may cut it in slices for four or five days afterwards, and it will be sweet and good for any use you may have for it, and garnish always with parsley.

TURKEY LARDED WITH BACON A LA GLASS

Dindon piqué au lard a la glass

Cut the pinions from your turkey, and the feet to the knee, and tuck into the skin of the thigh, flatten the breast well, and make a forcemeat with the livers and put in, cut some square pieces of bacon about two inches long, season with pepper, salt and spice, and lard your turkey, put it into a pot just big enough, and season with a carrot, an onion or two, herbs and spice, pepper, salt, and a bit of shallot, put in as much broth and water as will cover it, put over a slice or two of bacon, and let it simmer for two hours or more, let it cool and take out your fowl, pass off the broth, take the fat off, and order it as before, and serve it up; garnish with parsley, and this may serve for four or five days after.

HARE CAKE

Gateau de lievre

Take the flesh of a hare, and chop very fine, some bacon in dice about half the quantity, season with pepper, a little salt and spice, a green onion or two, and a morsel of shallot; mix all well together, and prepare a stewpan just wide enough, that it may cut in slices about two inches thick, line your bottom with thin bacon, and cover with the same, pour in a ladle of broth, and a glass of red wine, some slices of carrot, onions and herbs; let it simmer gently for two or three hours, take off the cover and let it cool; the next day take it out and trim it nice and round, pound some of the bacon that it was stewed in, and when you serve it to table spread it upon the top like sugar upon a plumb-cake, and serve it to table garnished as before upon a napkin; if it is well done, it will keep a fortnight for slices.

Veal-cake, or *Gateau de veau*, in the same manner, only instead of red wine put white; and don't cover it so much but every one at table may see what it is.

A PARTRIDGE-PYE COLD, WITH FORCEMEAT

Un pate des perdreaux froid, a la farce

Four partridges will do very well for a good middle or end dish, and you may make either long or round; blanch them, and a forcemeat of the livers, &c., to put withinside; but to fill up your fry take a piece of lean mutton about a pound, take out the sinewy or skinny parts, and cut it in bits, the udder of a calf or such sort of fat, and cut some scraped bacon, a morsel of ham; fry this with a mushroom or truffle or two, some green onions, pepper, salt, spices and herbs, all minced; fry all together a few minutes, and when cool chop it and pound it to a paste, lay your birds upon a sheet of poor paste, upon plenty of paper, and fill the chasms with your forcemeat, put a little pepper and salt upon the birds, and cover with lards of bacon; make another thick sheet of paste and cover it; press it well at the bottom, that it may not leak; cut it even and twist round, make what ornament you like, but the French only use pastry pinchers all over; when it is well baked pour in a ladle of gravy and cullis well seasoned, stop the hole at top, and turn it upside down for a while that every part may be seasoned alike, and serve it up next day for a cold *entremet*.

The next and last thing except one I propose is, to shew the manner of the French in getting up their roast for second course; but shall say but little, because the old English way, in my opinion, is much to be preferred before it, both for goodness and beauty.

First of all, in trussing their *volailles*, or fowls of any sort, they take off the pinions and claws of every one; but I think it is wrong to deprive turkey-poults, fowls or chickens, or pigeons of them; but pheasants, partridges, woodcocks, snipes, or quails, is prettiest; next they lard almost all, as if bacon should be equally good sauce for a quail or a snipe as it is for a fowl or a chicken; they lard them all, that is, roast all in slices of bacon without the least distinguishment, which must be wrong again: they use no flour, or basting of any sort to give colour, and send no sauce to table in the dishes with them; but in boats or cups they do two or three sorts, them I shall put down before I finish. In short, let the French send over so many pretty *entremets* to table, their roast is apt to darken it all. They are roasted by guess; all are greasy; some roasted almost to a powder, and some not half done. Instances of this I have often seen.

The Sea Tortoise *or* Turtle

SAUCES

SAUCES

The three sauces are, *sauce pauvrade, sauce Robert*, and *sauce pauvre homme.*

POOR MAN'S SAUCE

Sauce de pauvre homme

To a large spoonful of good sharp vinegar put about as much water, some salt, plenty of shallot and parsley minced very fine, squeeze in the juice of a lemon or orange or two; stir it well together, and when your roast goes to table send it up in a boat or cup.

Sauce Robert

To a ladle of cullis put a glass of your best white wine, a spoonful of mustard, pepper, salt, shallots and parsley, with plenty of such sorts of herbs as you best approve on; let all stew a minute or two, squeeze in plenty of juice, and send it up hot in a boat.

Sauce pauvrade

This is like the last, only instead of cullis use a clear gravy, a spoonful of vinegar, and the same ingredients to season it; and you may boil it as long as you like, squeeze in a great deal of lemon or orange, and send it up as the others. The reason why the *sauce Robert* should not boil long, is, because mustard in boiling grows bitter, and of a nauseous taste.

My next and last is to shew the best method of dissecting, preparing, and dressing of a turtle.

I have seen many a one drest, but I think not all as they should be; and as I have the honour of sending several to table myself, to some of the politest gentry in the kingdom with great applause, shall give the following receipt from experience rather than from the general rule of hodge-podgeing it together. To dissect it then, let its head be chopt off close to the shell, set it on that part that all the blood may run away, have plenty of water in several pails or tubs, lay your fish upon the back or calliopash, cut off the under shell or calliopee, in the first line or partition, from the edge of the calliopash, take that off and immediately put it into water; next cut off the four fins in the shoulder and aich-bone joints, and put into water too, and with a cleaver chop out the bones from the shoulders and hinder parts, and put to the rest; take out your guts and tripe clean, and the other entrails, and lay your calliopash in water while you prepare your calliopee, which should be done as follows: Cut off all superfluous bits for your soup, and trim it neatly; cut little holes in the thick flesh, with the point of your knife; lay it in a dish and soak it well in Madeira wine, and season with Kian pepper (but not too much) a little salt, plenty of shallot and parsley minced and strewed upon it; next take the calliopash, and order in the same manner, first cutting off the shell to the screase on the other side of the edge, and put a neat rim of paste quite round, and adorn it well; pour a little cullis round, and squeeze the juice of some lemons or oranges and they are ready for your oven: the common way is to put some of the flesh into the calliopash, but in my opinion it is best to put none. The next to be made ready is your fins and head; blanch them till you can take off the outer skin, trim them, and put them into a stewpan with the head, pour in some Madeira, a ladle of broth, a pinch of Kian, a small bunch of onions, herbs, and shallots, and stew them tender with a little salt, and 'tis ready; the two biggest fins for one dish, and the head and two smallest for another; now cut the side shells in pieces, and blanch them so that you may take the gristles or jelly part out whole; while this is doing prepare the tripe or guts with a sharp knife, slit them from end to end; and care must be taken that all is washed and scraped clean, cut them into pieces about two inches in length, and blanch them; when your broth is made of the flesh, to the tripe in a stewpan put as much as will cover it, put in a bunch of herbs, with an onion or two, a couple of whole shallots, some mace, and a little salt, stew all till pretty tender; take out the herbs, &c., and put butter and flour to thicken it; provide a liaison as for a fricasee of chickens, and at your dinner-time toss it up with the juice of lemon or orange, and it is ready. Next take the jellies of your side shells, and prepare for a dish done in the same manner as the fins and the head, squeeze in some juice of orange or lemon, and it is ready. And now for the soup; most of which that I have seen or tasted has been poor insipid stuff; to say why it was is saying less than nothing. The whole matter is, to shew how it may be made good: thus they cut all the flesh from the bones into small pieces, and to about a pound of meat put a quart of water, and to five or six quarts a pint of Madeira; take care that it well skimmed; tie up in a bit of linen three of four onions, some bits of carrot, a leek, some herbs and parsley, with two or three pinches of Kian; and let it boil with the meat; add salt according to your taste; let it simmer an hour or a little more and send it up in a terrine or soup-dish only the meat and broth.

These seven dishes make a pretty first-course, the calliopash and calliopee at top and bottom, soup in the middle, and the other four the corners.

Rabbit.

GLOSSARY

Amlet	Omelette
Bouillion	Broth
Cardoon	Plant allied to an artichoke cultivated for its fleshy stalks of inner leaves, grown with earth or straw piled high so stalks remain white
Collops	Dishes made from meat cut into small pieces
Cullis Coulis	Basic brown sauce of meat stock thickened with flour and butter
Entrèe	A first course side dish or corner dish
Entremets	Side dishes
Etamine	Sieve, usually of fine cloth
Glass	Glacé
Grass	Asparagus
Hors d'oevres Hors d'ouvres	Small dishes served as a relish at the beginning of a meal, or between courses of a meal
Lardoons	Strips of fat used in larding

Maigre	Meatless dish or soup
Manchet	Finest kind of wheaten bread
Matelotte	Fish stew with wine
Morel Morelle	An edible fungus
Nantiles	Lentils
Nouilles	Paste of flour and egg cut in the same way as vermicelli
Pouvrade	Poivrade, pepper sauce
Prill	Brill
Rocombole	Rocambole, a kind of leek used for seasoning dishes, Spanish garlic, sand leek
Rowls	Rolls
Salamander	Long-handled implement used by cooks and bakers to brown pastry, potatoes, etc., and take rawness off eggs. Placed near the fire till red hot then held at a short distance from the top of the dish
Sallet	Salad
Sewet	Suet
Skillet	Small cooking vessel
Trevet Trivet	A three-footed stand for a cooking vessel
Water-Souchy	Fish soup

INDEX

INDEX

Cheese

Eggs

Fish

Fish *continued*

Ham

Mutton and Lamb

Pork

Poultry and Game

Poultry and Game *continued*

Sauces

Soups

Sweet dishes